THE PSALMS AS CHRISTIAN PRAISE

World Christian Books

A SERIES OF BOOKS COVERING THE WHOLE RANGE
OF THE CHRISTIAN FAITH IN THE MODERN WORLD

Edited by Bishop Stephen Neill

*Sponsored by the International Missionary Council
in co-operation with the Christian Literature
Council of Great Britain and the Committee on
World Literacy and Christian Literature of the
United States, and the Department of Overseas
Missions of the Canadian Council of Churches.
Published by the United Society for Christian
Literature and the Lutterworth Press, London.*

WORLD CHRISTIAN BOOKS

No. 24

THE PSALMS AS CHRISTIAN PRAISE

by

R. B. Y. SCOTT

UNITED SOCIETY FOR CHRISTIAN LITERATURE

LUTTERWORTH PRESS

London

Printed by Page Bros. (Norwich) Ltd.
Mile Cross Lane, Norwich

CONTENTS

NOTE

Quotations from the Psalms are taken chiefly from the Revised Standard Version, but occasionally they follow the Authorized Version, and in other instances have been translated or adapted by the author from the Hebrew.

Biblical references are numbered as in the English versions.

INTRODUCTION

When we open our Bible in the middle, we find that we have opened it at the Book of Psalms. This is suggestive, for in more ways than one the Psalms are the heart of the Bible. What the whole Bible means to the Christian believer, as the story of what God has done for our salvation and as a means of grace through which He continues to speak, that the Psalms mean in a very special way.

This is not to say that the Psalms are more important than the Gospels and Epistles, which tell what God has done for us in the life and death and resurrection of Jesus Christ. On the contrary, without these we should have no Christian Bible at all. Yet even the New Testament does not provide us, as the Psalms do, with the language of prayer and praise with which to express *our response* to the Gospel. The only New Testament passages which resemble them are the Song of Mary, the Prophecy of Zacharias and the Prayer of Simeon, in the first two chapters of St. Luke's Gospel. These are *Christian* Psalms which are modelled on the Psalms of the Old Testament. Of a rather different type are the great songs in the Book of Revelation.

This is the reason why, if one book from the Old Testament is selected to be bound up with the New Testament as a little Bible, it is the Book of Psalms. For here more than in any other part of the Bible we find language fitting and ready for our use in addressing the God and Father of our Lord Jesus Christ. We must have words to utter our prayers and thanksgiving, and here they are. This is a strange and wonderful thing because, as we know, these words were written by men who died

7

long before Jesus Christ was born. The same God whom we worship had spoken to them of His righteous will. He had shown to them His goodness and His saving power. They too were His people.

Our first reason for speaking of the Psalms as "Christian Praise" is that they are a central part of the self-revelation of God to His ancient people Israel. The New Testament would be sadly incomplete without the Old Testament. It would be like a tree without roots, or the climax of a story without the first part which leads up to it. The *New* Covenant or Testament is so called because God had made a former covenant with Israel His chosen people. The first Christians took over and made their own the sacred writings of the Jewish Church. Indeed, the Old Testament was the only Bible which the early Christians had until the Epistles and Gospels were written.

A second reason why we speak of the Psalms as *Christian* hymns and prayers is that, of all the Old Testament writings, they are the most readily "baptized into Christ". The Gospel story bears witness to the fact that our Lord Himself nourished His own spiritual life by meditation on the Psalms. Quotations from them came so easily to His lips that He must have known them by heart. They served as the channel of His intimate communion with God. In His cry of agony from the cross—"My God, my God, why hast thou forsaken me?" He was repeating the opening words of Psalm 22. A later verse of the same Psalm proved true—"When he cried unto Him, he heard".

Because, then, of their Lord's example and of their own experience of the spiritual truth and power of the Psalms, the earliest disciples began what the Church throughout all the world has continued to this day, their constant use in the worship of God. This was a natural thing to do. Yet soon it became evident that the old words had richer meaning for men and women who believed in Jesus. The trust which they affirmed had now a firmer foundation. The praise they uttered gained richer content. Their cry of need could now be addressed to the God who so loved the world that He had given His only-begotten Son that they might not perish.

Hence from the very beginnings and through all the history of the Christian Church the Psalms have been used and treasured. They are familiar in the worship services of all branches of the Church to-day. They are also the best aids to private devotion. The first Christians sang in thanksgiving "psalms and hymns and spiritual songs" (Col. 3 : 16), and since those days the Psalms have been the inspiration of the hymn writers of Christendom. Indeed, some of our greatest hymns are actually paraphrases of the Psalms; that is, their thought has been expressed more fully in the form of more modern verse. For example, "O God, our help in ages past" is a magnificent paraphrase of Psalm 90.

The special importance of the Psalms in the Bible is this—that it is the book of worship, of the words which God's servants speak to God.

It should not surprise anyone, therefore, to learn that these sacred poems were originally composed for this very purpose. Some were used in the formal priestly services of the temple; others were written for the simpler services of the "synagogue" which was without altar or animal sacrifice. The occasional references to forms of Jewish worship do not prevent the transfer of the Psalms to Christian ways of worship, in any age or land. For example, the phrase "the house of the LORD" referred in the first place to the sanctuary in Jerusalem. But it may equally well be taken to refer to any "house of God" where men worship Him in spirit and in truth.

Christianity is not merely a system of belief and a code of right behaviour. It is a *service* offered to God in grateful response to His love and humble obedience to His will. Belief and trust are the mainsprings of this service. Behaviour in daily life is right, when it reflects something of the goodness, the love and the truth of God. It is a proof of religious sincerity. But the total response of the Christian to the God who has redeemed him must find expression also in the spiritual act of worship.

The whole Bible tells the story of God's calling into being a people to be His People. It tells how "last of all He sent unto them His Son". Worship expresses our answer to what God has said and has done for us. We serve Him in life and in worship, in adoration and communion, and in our cry to Him in the hour of utmost need. In the Psalms our worship finds a voice. They help us when our words cannot utter what our hearts would say. Just as one of our number may lead us in prayer, and as a choir may lead in singing, so the psalmists lead our thoughts in prayer and praise. They show us how man may speak to God, as in the prophets and the Gospels and other parts of the Bible God has spoken and still speaks to man.

These saints of old may do even more for us. They teach us to pray, as our Lord also taught His disciples. They carry us into a wider world of spiritual experience than we had dreamed of. Our inward vision is purified and we become able to grasp more firmly the reality of spiritual things. The words they put into our mouths become true for us too, as we learn to lift up our eyes unto the hills from which cometh our help.

One of the most remarkable features of the Book of Psalms is the way in which it provides for the needs of the individual as well as those of our common worship. Each one of us is a unique person, a self distinct from all other selves. "Each one of us shall give account of *himself* to God". At the same time we are "members one of another", and cannot be fully ourselves in complete solitude. Hence our worship must be both individual and corporate. "I am poor and needy, yet the Lord thinketh upon *me*". "*We* are his people, and the sheep of his pasture".

The question may be asked—if the Psalms are so direct and universal in their appeal, why is a book about them necessary or even useful? St. Paul suggests the answer—"I will sing with the spirit; I will sing with the understanding also". The better we know and understand about this book of prayers and praises, and the more we learn about its history and meaning, the richer it should prove as a means of grace. There is another reason, of a different kind. Simple honesty compels us to admit that certain features of the Book of Psalms are puzzling, and others raise moral questionings in the Christian's mind. In some passages the meaning is obscure because of expressions or references that we do not understand. Moral problems arise when a psalmist utters a bitter cry of vengeance on his enemies, for our Lord has taught us to love our enemies and do good to those who use us wrongly and persecute us.

Those things that trouble the conscience must not be glossed over and ignored, and that which we claim to value must have our best attention and fullest understanding. This little handbook to "The Psalms as Christian Praise" is an attempt to help the reader of the Psalms to understand what the Psalms are, and how they came down to the Christian Church from ancient Israel. It also seeks to deal, as helpfully as may be, with some of the difficulties which we face when we take over for Christian use this ancient Hebrew manual of religious devotion.

parallelism. Sometimes one of the principal words of the first line is not actually repeated but is carried forward in the minds of the poet and his hearers.

> The LORD: is a great God,
> (and)   : a great King above all gods. (Psalm 95 : 3)

In Psalm 95 : 5 we have an example of a verse where a parallel is completed by balancing two phrases at the beginning and the end; both lines must be taken together to convey the thought:

> The sea is his: for he made it,
>   : for his hands formed: the dry land.

The sea and the dry land—the whole earth—are God's, for He is their Creator. So in Psalm 42 : 8 when one thing is said of the day and another of the night, the meaning is that both things are true continually:

> By day: the LORD commands his lovingkindness,
> And at night: his song is with me.

In many other ways a thought is echoed in successive lines or verses. In Psalm 29 the thrice-repeated "Ascribe unto the LORD . . ." is solemnly impressive; the thunder peals seven times in the words "the voice of the LORD" (compare Psalm 18 : 13).

Illustration by comparison is a favourite form of parallelism:

> As a hart longs: for flowing streams,
> So my soul longs: for thee, O God. (Psalm 42 : 1)

Sometimes the balancing idea is in contrast:

> In the morning it flourishes and is renewed,
> In the evening it fades and withers. (Psalm 90 : 6)

At other times the second line states what follows on the first:

> I waited patiently for the LORD;
> He inclined to me and heard my cry. (Psalm 40 : 1)

14

Once the reader has become accustomed to notice this feature of parallelism, he will find the many skilful variations of it an added ornament to the poet's song. More important, he will be saved from misunderstanding what the poet means, as he might do through slavish literalism.

A second point to be observed is that many Psalms are made up of distinct stanzas. With these the psalmist builds up a literary structure which combines the different elements of the message he wishes to convey. Psalm 1 is a good example. Verses 1–2 tell of the happiness of the man who finds his pleasure in the study of God's Law rather than in the company of wicked men. Verses 3–4 contrast his experience of life with that of the wicked, who are like dusty chaff blown away by the wind. The last two verses declare that the righteous and the wicked have opposite destinies, because the Lord judges them according to their character and deeds.

Sometimes the divisions between the stanzas is marked by refrains or by the Hebrew word *Selah* (about which something will be said later). In Psalm 46 we have three stanzas, marked by a *Selah* after verse 3 and by a refrain in verses 7 and 11. Psalms 42 and 43 form one poem which for some reason was divided by the editors into two; we can see that there are three stanzas of equal length concluding with the same refrain.

Many Psalms, however, do not display regularity of form. In some there is no clear mark of division into different parts, and in others the length of the stanzas varies. The number of lines, and the number of important words in a single line do not follow a rigid pattern. The poets retain their freedom to create their poems in their own way, and seldom do two Psalms show exactly the same literary structure.

In addition to parallelism, an important literary

feature of the Psalms is the vividness of the imagery drawn from daily life to illustrate the thought. The bare rocky hills of Palestine are always in view (Psalms 121 : 1; 125 : 2), some of them crowned with grim fortresses (Psalm 71 : 3). The open valleys are green with growing crops, and the slopes are dotted here and there with flocks of sheep (Psalm 65 : 13). Westward lies the sea, glowing in the sunlight or lashed by the fury of the storm (Psalm 104 : 25–26). When thunder roars, it is like the voice of God, and the earth trembles (Psalm 29). In the drought of summer the hot wind raises the dust from paths trodden by men and animals, and whirls the chaff from the threshing-floor (Psalm 1 : 4). The quiet pool at the spring is like the water of life (Psalm 23 : 2). When night comes, the stars are brilliant (Psalm 8 : 1–4).

Along the winding paths between village and village people pass continually, often in danger of attack (Psalm 27 : 11). The judge upon his seat hears the complaint of those who have been robbed, or who are falsely accused (Psalm 58 : 11). We see the shepherd with his staff (Psalm 23 : 1, 4), the hunter with his net (Psalm 35 : 7–8), the harvester returning from the field (Psalm 126 : 6), the chieftain in his tent entertaining a guest (Psalm 23 : 6), the musician with harp and lyre (Psalm 57 : 8), and the bridegroom on his wedding day (Psalm 19 : 5). An army with banners goes out to battle, the soldiers carrying bows and arrows, swords and shields, and the chariot-horses ready to strike terror into the enemy (Psalms 20 : 5, 7; 76 : 3). Processions move through the streets to the portals of the temple on "the holy hill" (Psalms 24 : 7–10; 68 : 24–25). The priests encircle the smoking altar while the congregation stands watching in the courtyard of the temple (Psalm 118 : 27). There is the sound of chanting from the choir, and the people answer with a united cry of petition or of praise (Psalm 118 : 1–4). In the homes of the people a lamp is lit at evening (Psalm 18 : 28), and a mother nurses her child (Psalm 8 : 2). Someone stumbles, and precious water is spilt on the ground (Psalm 22 : 14). A jar is dropped and shattered (Psalm 2 : 9). In the darkness evildoers are abroad (Psalm 11 : 2), and the sick man tosses on his bed until dawn (Psalm 22 : 14–15).

By sketching such pictures from life the poet expresses his feelings and illustrates his thought. He cries to God in agony:

> I am poured out like water . . .
> My heart is like wax melted within me,
> My strength is dried up like a potsherd. (Psalm 22 : 14–15)

His despair gives him the feeling that he is sinking,

> . . . sinking in deep mire where there is no foothold,
> I am in deep water, and the flooding stream sweeps over me.
> (Psalm 69 : 2)

Hope in God is pictured in images of security:

> He will hide me in his shelter in the day of trouble;
> He will conceal me in his tent;
> He will put me high upon a rock. (Psalm 27 : 5)

To another psalmist God is, above all, his place of refuge—

> Though the earth should change,
> Though the mountains shake in the heart of the sea.
> (Psalm 46 : 2)

The seas and hills are pictured as rejoicing like happy people at God's coming:

> Let the floods clap their hands!
> Let the hills sing for joy together! (Psalm 98 : 8)

Through God's blessing—

> The meadows are clothed with flocks,
> The valleys are decked with grain;
> They shout and sing together for joy. (Psalm 65 : 13)

But the hot sun of summer can smite like an enemy, unless—

> The LORD is your shade on your right hand. (Psalm 121 : 5)

Men's lives pass swiftly—

> They are like a dream,
> Like grass which is renewed in the morning . . .
> By evening it fades and withers. (Psalm 90 : 5–6)

The use of pictorial language is particularly notable when the poets speak of God. Their figures of speech are meant to suggest far more than can be put into words.

He who sits in the heavens is laughing at the plots of kings and rulers; He will speak to them in His wrath (Psalm 2 : 4–5). The LORD looks down from heaven upon the children of men, to see if there are any that act wisely (Psalm 14 : 2). He will break the teeth of the wicked (Psalm 3 : 7). His eyes behold, His eyelids test the children of men (Psalm 11 : 4). He will "incline his ear" to those who trust Him, but will "hide his face" from sinners. In the description of the tempest in Psalm 18 : 7–15 it is said that, when God was angry, smoke went up from His nostrils and devouring fire from His mouth.

Do these descriptions mean that the psalmists really thought of God as having a body like the body of a man, with eyes, hands, feet, face, nostrils and mouth? When they say that God was angry, contemptuous, tender, purposeful or pleased, does this mean that He has the characteristic emotions of men? When He is called a judge, a king, a shepherd, a father, or is pictured as a soldier sharpening his sword, what is the poet trying to say?

The first thing to be remembered is that this is poetry, not prose. The poet paints these pictures in order to suggest what he means by appealing to our imagination. The protecting strength of God is conveyed by the figure of a rock, a shadow or a fortress. The LORD God

18

is a sun and shield (Psalm 84 : 11). As the mountains are round about Jerusalem, so the LORD is round about His people (Psalm 125 : 2).

This last verse makes it clear that all these word-pictures, including those drawn from the human form and human emotions, are simply poetic ways of speaking of man's experience of God. The reasons that God is here pictured in language drawn from human experience are two: "no man hath seen God at any time"; and, God's relationship to man is *like* that of a shepherd to his flock, a king to his subjects, a father to his children. Men speak to Him in prayer as they might to a ruler or a judge, acknowledging their faults, praising His goodness and asking for His aid, yet with reverence and awe such as no earthly potentate could evoke.

> When I look at thy heavens, the work of thy fingers,
> The moon and the stars which thou hast established;
> What is man that thou art mindful of him?
> O LORD, our Lord, how majestic is thy name in all the earth!
> (Psalm 8 : 3–4, 9)

> O LORD, my God, thou art very great!
> Thou coverest thyself with light as with a garment!
> (Psalm 104 : 1, 2)

> If I take the wings of the morning
> And dwell in the uttermost parts of the sea,
> Even there thy hand shall lead me. (Psalm 139 : 9, 10)

This is the pure essence of religion, clothed in the speech of poetry.

A Service-Book of the Jewish Church

The Book of Psalms is not simply a collection of religious poems compiled for private use. It is the latest edition of a combined prayer-book and hymn-book containing many forms of worship used in ancient Israel. It has been called "the Hymn-book of the

Second Temple", that is, of the Jerusalem temple which had been destroyed and was restored after the Babylonian Exile of the Jews (586-538 B.C.).

This title is only partly correct, for two reasons. The Psalm-Book contains many poems which do not fall naturally into the class of "hymns", even though "Praises" is the title given to them in the Hebrew Bible as we have it to-day. There are prayers of entreaty and confession, litanies, ritual forms, and devotional meditations which demand a broader descriptive title such as "Service Book" or "Forms of Worship". The second reason is that some, at least, of these poems come down from older, pre-Exilic sanctuaries, not only at Jerusalem but at Shiloh (1 Sam. 1 : 3), Bethel (Amos 5 : 23; 7 : 13), and other places. Other Psalms, such as the long meditation on the Law, Psalm 119, can hardly have been used in temple worship at all. It is evident from the inclusion of these that the Psalm-Book was given its final form for use in the worship of the synagogues rather than that of the temple. The synagogues were originally local gatherings for study of Scripture and informal worship by those who could not be present at the temple.

Many of the Psalms, however, do go back to the time at which the temple was standing. The legal and historical books of the Old Testament give us some pictures of the way in which the sacrificial worship of the sanctuary was carried on, and these are supplemented by glimpses of it in the prophetic books. Again and again there is reference to "the songs of the temple" (Amos 8 : 3), and to words of prayer and praise which remind us of the Psalms.

Deuteronomy 26 : 1-10 lays down both the words and the acts of the ceremony for the farmer's presentation of the "first fruits" at the sanctuary. What the farmer is to repeat after the priest (vss. 5–10) is similar to Psalm 105. In Deuteronomy 21 : 1–9 appears the ceremony for protesting innocence of crime. Psalm 26 has the same theme, though the crime is different. We notice in both the symbolic washing of the hands. In another connection, the priestly blessing in Numbers 6 : 22–27 is recalled by the language of Psalms 20 : 1; 118 : 26; and 134 : 3.

Hannah's agonized prayer and vow in 1 Samuel 1 : 10–11 have their counterparts in Psalm 22, where the psalmist likewise pledges himself to pay the vow he makes in his distress. Indeed, there are several references in the Psalms to the payment of such vows (50 : 14; 65 : 1; 66 : 13–14). At the dedication of the temple, described in 1 Kings 8, Solomon speaks of the prayers which would be made before the altar in various circumstances, and to these different types of Psalms correspond; cf. 1 Kings 8 : 33–34 and Psalm 106 : 6.

In the narrative of the foundation of the second temple, we read that the priests and Levites sang responsively, "giving thanks to the LORD, for he is good, for his mercy endures forever" (Ezra 3 : 10–11). This refrain will be recognized at once by anyone familiar with the Psalms, where it occurs again and again. Indeed, in Psalms 118 : 1–4 and 136 its use as a liturgical refrain is striking. In Jeremiah 33 : 11 we are told that this was what men sang as they brought the thankoffering to the house of the Lord. Jeremiah 31 : 6 gives the keynote of the Psalms of festival pilgrimage, "Arise, and let us go up to Zion": cf. Psalm 122 : 1— "I was glad when they said to me, Let us go to the house of the LORD". Isaiah 1 : 11–15 associates prayer with outstretched hands with temple sacrifice. Joel twice refers to a service of lamentation and entreaty, when the priests, clad in sackcloth, prayed almost in the words of Psalm 79 (cf. Joel 1 : 13–14; 2 : 12-17).

In the Psalm-Book itself are indications that some, and probably many, of these poems were composed originally for use in the temple. Psalm 24 : 7–10 is evidently the ritual of solo and chorus which was used when the ark was carried in procession through the gate of the temple. In Psalm 20 it is possible to identify the part spoken by the presiding priest (vss. 1–4), the army or congregation (vs. 5), and a prophet or the king himself (vss. 6–9). In Psalm 118 : 2–4 the threefold response of *Israel* (the congregation), of *the house of Aaron* (the priests), and of *those who fear the* LORD (the proselytes, or, all present) is called for. In this 118th Psalm, indeed, several "rubrics" (directions for conducting the ceremony) have in the present form of the Psalm been merged with the words to be spoken. The triumphant shout of the people in verses 15–16 is entitled "the sound of the victory shout". The second half of verse 27 is another rubric which has crept into the text from the margin; if the words are put in brackets the text of the Psalm is not interrupted.

Thus a Psalm often is more clearly understood when we recognize that it was originally meant to accompany a temple ceremony. In Numbers 15 : 3, 8 the payment of a vow is listed as one of the occasions when sacrifices were offered. In Psalm 66 : 13–15 we have the words uttered by a man who came to the temple to pay such a vow, followed by his public acknowledgment to all present that God had given him the deliverance for which he prayed. In another Psalm the worshipper, as he pays his vows, lifts up "the cup of salvation", so called because it was the cup from which the accompanying drink-offering was poured out in gratitude for God's deliverance (Psalm 116 : 13–14; cf. Num. 15 : 5).

The ritual prescribed for the sin-offering in Numbers 19 : 17–18 explains the phrase "purge me with hyssop" in Psalm 51 : 7. In Psalm 81 : 2–3 we hear the music and trumpets sounding at the New Year festival. The hand-clapping (cf. 2 Kings 11 : 12), the shouting and the sounding of trumpets at New Year appear again in Psalm 47. The whole orchestra of the temple service accompanies the final burst of praise which concludes the Psalm-Book (Psalm 150).

Many, though not all, of the Psalms thus come to us from the ancient ritual service of the temple at Jerusalem. Later they were adapted, as we have seen, for use in the more informal worship of the synagogue. The temple with its hereditary priesthood, its animal sacrifices and strange ceremonies, has long passed away. But the spiritual reality and genuine devotion of these ancient prayers and hymns has been preserved for the worship of God through the ages.

We must remember, however, that not all the Psalms written in ancient Israel were collected into the Book of Psalms; as we shall see later, some were inserted here and there in the historical books and the books of the prophets. Furthermore, Psalms continued to be written after the Old Testament was completed. From shortly before the birth of Christ comes a collection of eighteen Psalms which someone entitled "Psalms of Solomon" because King Solomon is said in 1 Kings 4 : 32 to have composed many "songs". These are modelled on the Psalms in the Bible, but reflect later beliefs such as that in the resurrection of the dead; the 3rd Psalm of Solomon says:

> But they that fear the Lord shall rise to life eternal,
> And their life shall be in the light of the Lord, and shall come to an end no more.

In the first two chapters of St. Luke's Gospel are the

three canticles or songs, "Magnificat", "Benedictus" and "Nunc Dimittis" which in form and content closely resemble the Old Testament Psalms. We may note that the Angel's words to Zechariah (Luke 1 : 14–17) and to Mary (Luke 1 : 32–33, 35) and the heavenly anthem (Luke 2 : 14) are also in poetic form.

Among the Dead Sea Scrolls which have come to light in recent years from the library of a Jewish sect in Palestine in the time of Jesus are some "Thanksgivings" which remind us a little of the biblical Psalms. They do not appear to be hymns for congregational worship, however, but rather an individual's prayers and confessions of faith. Their form is closer to prose than to poetry. But, as may be seen from the following sample, they express a real piety which has been nurtured on the Bible:

> I praise thee, O my God, for thou has dealt wonderfully
>   with dust,
> And with one moulded of clay thou hast shown thy power.
> Though I am praising thee, what am I?
> For it is thou who hast given me knowledge of thy true counsel.
> And hast made me to understand thy wonderful acts,
> And hast put confession in my mouth, and (a song) on my
>   tongue,
> And ready speech in the abode of loud rejoicing.
> So I will hymn thy mercies and meditate on thy power all
>   through the day;
> Continually will I bless thy name.
> I will declare thy glory among the sons of men,
> and in the abundance of thy goodness my soul shall delight.
> For I know that thy mouth is truth, in thy hand is
> righteousness, in thy thoughts is all knowledge, in
> thy might is all strength, and with thee is all glory.
>   (Thanksgiving Scroll, col. 11, lines 3–8)

CHAPTER TWO

WHAT THE PSALM-BOOK CONTAINS

The Christian must know his way round in the Psalm-Book if he is to make the best use of it as a means of religious devotion. This requires something more than knowing the numbers of his favourite Psalms. Some Psalms have become general favourites because they express so clearly and beautifully what the reader believes and wishes to say. There are many others which can become deeply meaningful only after the effort to understand them has been made.

Such effort is particularly needful, as one reads the Psalms in order from beginning to end of the collection. We are bound to ask why, for example, a Psalm differs so much in subject matter and mood from the one which precedes it and the one which follows it (cf. Psalm 2). Why, further, are there sometimes such abrupt changes within a single poem, as in Psalm 19? Is there any reason for the order in which the Psalms follow each other? Why are Psalms 120-134 grouped together and called "Songs of Ascents"? What do the headings like "A Maskil of Ethan the Ezrahite" (Psalm 89) mean, and why do so many Psalms lack such introductions? Why are some called "Psalms of David" and others not?

Some of these questions may appear more important to scholars who are trying to trace the history of the growth of the Psalm-Book than to lay-people who want guidance in the religious use of this book. Here we shall touch only on some of the principal things which should be noticed by those who wish to read the Psalm-Book intelligently.

The Arrangement of the Psalm-Book

The Psalm-Book contains 150 Psalms, divided into five sections or "books", like the five "Books of Moses". It will be noticed that these are not of equal length, as might have been expected from the division of the round number 150. Each of them, except the fifth, ends with a similar doxology; the doxology, therefore, is not part of the Psalm to which in each case it has been attached, but is from the hand of the compilers who made the division into five parts. The fifth section requires no added doxology because Psalm 150 is itself a doxology. There is an additional note in Psalm 72 : 20 at the end of Book 2 : "The prayers of David, the son of Jesse, are ended".

These evidences of editorial arrangement point to the further fact that the editors have made a *selection* from a larger number of Psalms in order to limit the collection to the round number 150. The Old Greek version adds Psalm 151 and labels it "outside the number". Several other Psalms have been inserted by editors in the books of the prophets, at what seemed suitable points. Habakkuk 3 not only resembles Psalms 18 and 29 in its subject matter, but has a heading and a conclusion which show that it had at one time been included in a Psalm-Book. The "Writing of Hezekiah" in Isaiah 38 : 9–20 recalls the prayer of the sick man in Psalm 6. It, too, has a heading like those of the Psalm-Book, and the final verse shows that it was used in temple worship. Other Psalms are to be found scattered through the Old Testament—in Exodus 15; Deuteronomy 32; 1 Samuel 2; 2 Samuel 22; Isaiah 12, and Jonah 2. The Book of Lamentations is a little Psalm-Book in itself.

26

One of these additional Psalms which appears in 1 Chronicles 16 shows how Psalms or parts of Psalms were combined by the editors. This consists of Psalm 105 : 1–15, followed by Psalm 96, and the opening and closing verses of Psalm 106. In the Psalm-Book itself, similarly, certain Psalms have been put together by combining all or parts of other poems. The first part of Psalm 108 is taken from Psalm 57, the second part from Psalm 60. Psalm 70 reappears as the concluding section of Psalm 40. Psalm 14 and Psalm 53 are the same, except that in the latter "God" is substituted for "the LORD", with a few other minor differences.

What this means is that the present number of 150 has been obtained by certain rearrangements of the original material that the editors had before them. Psalms 19, 24, 27, 40 and others are the result of combining material from two or more original poems. Psalms 42 and 43 are clearly one composition divided into two. Recognition of this simple fact is often of assistance in our attempt to follow the thought of the poet in any particular Psalm. In Psalm 19, the first part tells of the revelation of God through the wonders of the sky, and the second part speaks of the Scriptures, which also reveal God, but in a very different way. This similarity explains why two Psalms so different in form have been combined.

The Collecting of the Psalms

The division of the final collection into five parts is like the divisions made in modern hymn-books by the committee which prepares them. In these hymn-books, hymns are brought together from many sources and previous collections, ancient and modern. Sometimes not only the names and dates of the author and the musical composer are given, but also the name of the older hymn-book in which the composition first appeared. If we observe carefully the contents of each of the five divisions of the Psalm-Book, we can learn something—though not as much as we should like—about the sources from which it has been put together.

The first thing to be noticed is that many of the Psalms appear in groups which are distinguished either by similarity of subject matter or by their headings. In Book 1 all except Psalms 1, 2 and 33 are marked "of David". In Books 2 and 3, Psalms 51–65 and 68–70 form a second "Davidic" group inserted in a collection headed by names of the choral guilds (groups of temple-singers) Korah, Asaph and Ethan. Another distinct group clearly marked by headings is Psalms 120–134, the "Songs of Ascents", that is, the "goings-up" to the temple in procession or pilgrimage.

Other Psalms seem to have been brought together because of similarity of subject. Psalms 93–99 dwell on the thought of the Lord as King and Judge of all the earth. Psalms 103–107 resemble one another as hymns of praise and thanksgiving. Psalms 111–113, 115–117 and 146–150 begin or end with "Hallelujah—Praise the LORD!" The Psalms with the refrain "for his mercy endureth forever" (100, 106, 107, 118, and 136) are, like these other groups, found only in Books 4 and 5. This is one reason for thinking that this final part of the Psalm-Book, Psalms 90–150, had originally been one single collection, and was divided in two when the fivefold division was made.

Unless we recognize that Books 1, 2–3 and 4–5 contain separate collections of Psalms which were put together to form our Psalm-Book, it is hard to explain why Psalm 14 in Book 1 should be repeated in Book 2 as Psalm 53. Other duplications occur, as already noted, but never in the same section of the Psalm-Book.

Another difference which can be explained from the combining of smaller collections is illustrated by comparing Psalms 14 and 53. In Psalm 14 the divine name "Jehovah—the LORD" is used three times; each time Psalm 53 changes it to the general Hebrew word for "God". In different religious circles and at different times, men were accustomed to use one or other name for God, just as in different translations of the Bible today the same Hebrew name is sometimes translated "Jehovah", sometimes "the LORD", and sometimes "The Eternal". This must be the reason why in Books 2 and 3 the name "God" is found about four times as often as the name "Jehovah—the LORD", whereas in the rest of the Psalm-Book the latter is used about twenty times as often as the former.

This recognition that smaller and older Psalm-Books once existed and were drawn upon in the compiling of the final collection explains how still other Psalms come to be scattered through other parts of the Bible. It explains also the statement in Psalm 72 : 20 that "the Psalms of David are ended" as referring to a Davidic collection which ended at that point, since other Davidic Psalms follow (86, 101, 103, 108–110, 122, 124, 131, 138–145). Finally, it gives us a clue to the meaning of the headings or titles with which most of the Psalms are introduced.

The Headings

These headings or titles are not part of the poems, but are notes about them inserted by ancient editors. The fact that 116 Psalms have headings and 34 do not is itself of interest. Some of the "orphans" (as the Psalms without headings have been called) occur singly, others in groups. A reason usually can be suggested for those which occur singly. Psalm 1 is an introduction to the whole collection. Psalms 10 and 43 are really parts of the Psalms immediately preceding. Psalm 33 has been attached to Psalm 32 as a sequel to its final verse. The "orphan Psalms" which are found in groups are all in Books 4–5, and are distinguished also by their subject matter and literary style (see Psalms 93–97, 99; 104–107; 111–118; 135–137; 146–150).

Several of the distinct items which make up the headings also occur chiefly in groups of Psalms, as well as singly. This is further evidence that we have to do with smaller Psalm-Books, some with headings and some without them, which have been brought together in our present collection.

1. *Descriptive terms* like "psalm", "song", "prayer", which classify the following poems and suggest the purpose which they served. A PSALM, strictly speaking, was a hymn sung by the temple choir to the accompaniment of musical instruments. Like our word "hymn", it meant primarily a song in praise of God, but came to include religious songs of other types as well. The title SONG seems to have the special sense of a processional hymn sung by the laity as they "entered his gates with thanksgiving, and his courts with praise". A picture of such a procession is given in Psalm 68 : 24–27 : "the singers in front, the minstrels last, between them maidens playing timbrels". The twelve poems which are entitled both "psalm" and "song" may have been used both in the processions and in the temple service.

Five Psalms are entitled "a PRAYER". All are of the same kind, as Psalm 102 where the title is expanded to "a prayer of one afflicted, when he is faint and pours out his complaint before the LORD". They make no reference to singing, so it is evident that they were prayers used by individual worshippers who came into the temple, like Hezekiah, to implore God's mercy (see Isaiah 37). Since Psalm 142 is called a PRAYER and also a MASKIL, it seems that a Maskil was a prayer for divine enlightenment. A MIKTAM (Psalms 16, 56–60) was probably a form of prayer for God's protection, associated with a vow to offer a sacrifice. The only example of a SHIGGAION (Psalm 7), is a prayer—presumably also accompanied by a sacrifice—that God will bring to light the wickedness of evildoers, and show that His worshipper is in the right in his dispute with them.

2. *Names of persons* associated with the Psalm which follows. Seventy-three Psalms are associated with David, fifty-five with "the choirmaster", twelve with Asaph, eleven with "the sons of Korah", and smaller numbers with Moses, Solomon, Heman, Ethan and Jeduthun. Moses, David and Solomon are well known from the early history of Israel. Who are the others, and what does it mean when a Psalm is entitled "of David" or "of the sons of Korah"?

These items in the headings, like the descriptive terms "psalm", "song" or "Maskil", seem to have something to do with the use of the Psalms in the musical services of the temple. All these names except Moses and Solomon are mentioned in the accounts in 1 Chronicles 6, 15 and 16 of David's arrangements for the musical services. Both Moses and Solomon are remembered as having composed songs (Exodus 15 : 1; Deuteronomy 31 : 22; 1 Kings 4 : 32). David was not only a poet (2 Samuel 1 : 17–27; 23 : 1–7) but a musician (1 Samuel 16 : 23). It is probable, therefore, that the heading "of David", like the headings "of Asaph" and "of the sons of Korah", referred originally to the fact that the Psalm came from a collection bearing the name of a famous singer of ancient times. This does not necessarily mean that he was the author, as is clear from "David" Psalms which speak of Solomon's temple as already in existence (Psalm 65 : 4), and the destruction of Jerusalem at the time of the Exile as already in the past (Psalm 51 : 18).

The tradition that David was "the sweet psalmist of Israel" (2 Samuel 23 : 1) is very ancient, and in thirteen Psalms (cf. Psalm 3) someone has added notes to the titles connecting them with some experience of David's life. The heading of Psalm 34 refers to David's feigning madness before a Philistine king as in 1 Samuel 21: 10–15, though the king's name is not the same in the two passages. These notes, of course, are not part of the Psalms themselves. They show us that the scribes of old, like the modern Bible student, tried to learn something about the writer of a Psalm and his circumstances by studying the Psalm itself, and wrote down their notes in the margin. Fortunately, the spiritual value and authority of the Psalms do not depend on our being able to identify with certainty the human author through whom God spoke. David undoubtedly wrote Psalms, but since the headings which mention his name refer to the use of the Psalms in the temple services rather than to authorship, we cannot say that in every case they point to him as the writer.

The "choirmaster" ("director", "chief musician") is mentioned in the headings almost as often as David. This word means "leader" or "overseer", but it is used in the account of David's arrangements for the musical services of the temple (1 Chronicles 15 : 21) not of an individual but of an orchestra. Psalm 150 : 3–5 names the instruments of this orchestra. From 1 Chronicles 15 : 16 and 16 : 41–42 we learn that those who played the instruments also led the singing.

3. *Musical directions* for the rendering of the Psalms as part of the temple services. All twenty-eight of these appear in headings which also are marked "for the orchestra". Unfortunately, the meaning of most of them is uncertain. Psalms 4, 6, 54, 55, 61, 67 and 76 were to be sung "with the playing of stringed instruments", though why this is said of only seven Psalms we do not know. All the other musical directions seem to refer, not to the musical instruments, but to the tune, rhythm or tone to be used. Psalm 22, for example, was sung to the tune or rhythm of a song called "the Hind of Dawn", and Psalm 56 to "the Dove of the Distant Terebinths". The term used in the heading of Psalm 5 means perhaps "the Flute Song", that in Psalm 6 "Song of the Fertile Land", and that in Psalms 8, 81 and 84 "Song of the Wine-press". The people's songs at the harvest of field and vineyard are known from other parts of the Bible (see Isaiah 5 : 1; 9 : 3; 16 : 10; 27 : 2). Certain Psalms were thus sung to popular melodies.

The Hebrew word *Selah* which is found one or more times in the body of many Psalms, rather than in the headings, is also a musical direction. It is like the words "chorus" and "refrain", which sometimes are written in brackets in modern hymns or secular songs to indicate that all those present are to join the soloist or choir in singing a short repeated line or verse. It means probably "lift up the voice here". In Psalms 3 and 46 we have good examples of *Selah* occurring at regular intervals to mark a refrain. In other Psalms it is found only at the point where the people were called on to join in a shout of entreaty or acclamation (24 : 10; 47 : 4; 66 : 8).

4. *Assignments to special occasions* or purposes in worship. Psalm 30 was marked to be sung at the annual

festival celebrating the dedication or rededication of the temple. Psalm 92 was used in the Sabbath services. Psalm 100 accompanied the sacrifice of thanksgiving, as we observe in Jeremiah 33 : 11, "those who sing, as they bring thank offerings to the house of the LORD: 'Give thanks to the LORD of hosts, for the LORD is good, for his mercy endures forever' ". Psalms 38 and 70 are designated "for the memorial offering" of which we read in Leviticus 24 : 7. The fifteen Psalms 120–134 are marked for use in processions going up to the house of the Lord.

Different Types of Psalms

The assignment of certain Psalms to special occasions in the worship of the temple draws our attention to the fact that they are of different types. The suitability of Psalm 100 to accompany the sacrifice of thanksgiving is obvious. We do not need the heading of Psalm 102 in order to see that it is "a prayer of one afflicted".

Thus, as we read through the Psalm-Book with close attention, we become aware that other Psalms resemble 100 and 102 in purpose and language. We begin to make our own classification. Even though such Psalms are not marked for use on occasions of public thanksgiving or private entreaty, we see that they could be used on such occasions equally well with those which are so designated.

In attempting to classify the Psalms, we must again remember two things. First, these sacred poems do not come down to us *directly* from the temple service books. They were taken over into the non-sacrificial worship of the synagogue, and were modified and added to, just as our modern hymn-books contain material both ancient and modern combined and adapted for use to-day. Psalms such as 1 and 119 can have had nothing

34

to do with sacrificial worship, but reflect the period when "the Law" (that is, the first Jewish Bible, the Law of Moses) rather than the altar of sacrifice was becoming the focal point of worship and private devotion.

The second point is one to which attention has already been drawn. In this combining of old and new material, some of the old Psalms have been rearranged and combined. As we attempt to take note of and classify the different types of Psalms we shall find, therefore, that sometimes we must recognize as a distinct poem what is now part of a longer Psalm.

1. *Psalms of Public Thanksgiving* like 100 are the first group. We notice here the reference to the congregation praising God in the courts of the temple because He is the Maker and Shepherd of His people. The last verse is a refrain which the people sang upon such occasions in the temple (see Psalms 106 : 1; 107 : 1; 118 : 1, 29, and especially Jeremiah 33 : 11 and the whole of Psalm 136). Psalm 65 is a thanksgiving for the privilege of worship, for God's power seen in nature and in history, and for the fruits of the earth. Psalm 75 praises God for His righteous judgments. These Public Thanksgivings resemble the Hymns of Praise, but are distinguished by the fact that they refer to particular acts of divine deliverance. Psalm 48, for example, seems to mark the deliverance from a threat to Jerusalem, such as that of Sennacherib (2 Kings 18, 19).

2. *General hymns of praise* of the greatness and goodness of God are found in their most typical form in Psalms 145–150. The title "Hymn of Praise" in 145 may have been intended to apply to the series of six Psalms, to be sung antiphonally by two choirs. Psalms 111–113, 115–117 begin or end: "Hallelujah—Praise the LORD!"

35

In 1 Chronicles 23: 30–31 we read that such hymns were sung in the temple morning and evening, and when burnt offerings were made on festivals.

Two other types of hymns must be mentioned here: the praise of God as Creator and Lord of nature, Psalms 8, 29 and 19 : 1–6; and the "new songs" which celebrated the divine sovereignty over all nations (Psalms 47, 93, 95).

3. *Songs of the Chosen People* express Israel's faith in "the God of Jacob" who is forever her "very present help". The holy city of Zion and its temple are loved as the place of His worship and the symbol of His saving power. "How lovely is thy dwelling place, O LORD of hosts!" (Psalm 84 : 1). The undying memory of what God has done in delivering Israel from Egypt is the ground of assurance for all time (Psalm 114). "Our help is in the name of the LORD, who made heaven and earth" (Psalm 124 : 8). Among other hymns of the covenant faith are Psalms 46, 48, 76, 87 and 122.

4. *Psalms of the Monarchy* point to temple ceremonies in which the king took part. When David brought the Ark to Jerusalem he was garbed as a priest and offered sacrifices (2 Samuel 6 : 14). 1 Kings 8 : 5–22, 62–64 pictures Solomon as officiating at the dedication of the temple. Psalm 110 : 4 speaks of the king as "a priest forever after the order of Melchizedek". This Psalm, like Psalm 2, shows that the king was thought of as standing in a unique relationship to God, ruling in His name. Psalms 72 and 132 seem to be prayers offered on the occasion of a king's accession to the throne. Psalm 45 celebrates a royal marriage. Psalm 20 is a prayer, and Psalm 21 a prophecy that the king will have victory in battle.

5. *Entreaties of the Community* when in distress can be recognized in such Psalms as 44, 79 and 80. In times of national danger or calamity, such as those named in Solomon's prayer in 1 Kings 8 : 33-40, 44-53, a fast was proclaimed and a solemn assembly was held at the temple. King, priests and people covered themselves with rough sackcloth and ashes (Isaiah 37 : 1; 58 : 5) and humbled themselves before God begging for deliverance. In the prophecy of Joel this service of agonized prayer and self-humiliation is described (Joel 1 : 15-20; 2 : 12-17). The warning trumpet sounds, the whole community gathers, and "between the vestibule and the altar the priests, the ministers of the LORD, weep and say, Spare thy people, O LORD!" There follow in 1 : 13-20 and 2 : 17 the words of the prayers of supplication. The first tells of a dreadful drought. The second uses language very similar to that of Psalms 44 and 79: "Make not thy heritage a reproach, a by-word among the nations. Why should they say among the peoples, Where is their God?" Jeremiah 14 : 2-9 similarly describes the disastrous results of a drought and concludes with a prayer for mercy.

Psalms 74 and 79 also are concerned with the desolation of the sanctuary wrought by an enemy. Psalm 44 marks a day of defeat in battle: "Thou hast not gone out with our armies; Thou hast made us turn back from the foe" (vss. 9-10; see 1 Kings 8 : 33-34). In Psalm 83 the nation is under threat of destruction, as when King Hezekiah went in sackcloth to the temple to implore the help of the Lord while the arrogant boasting of the King of Assyria rang in his ears (Isaiah 37 : 1-21). Psalm 80 is another prayer in similar circumstances.

6. *Prayers of entreaty by individuals in distress* are the

next class to be observed. One of the wonderful things about the religion of the Bible is that the individual is not lost in the mass. "The Lord takes thought for *me*" (Psalm 40 : 17). "Even the hairs of your head are all numbered" (Matthew 10 : 30).

We find many examples of such prayers in the Psalm-Book. Some are petitions for help in the struggle against personal enemies, for example, Psalms 3, 13 and 54. Psalm 28 has in view the treachery of false friends. Other Psalms cry out for the vindication of the innocent against his accusers—Psalms 17; 26; 35; 43; 64 and 71. Psalm 56 asks for the gift of courage. In several Psalms the writer is very ill and prays for deliverance from death—6, 31, 102. Again, the psalmist feels that God has forsaken him—22, 42, 77. The deepest need is that for God's forgiveness and cleansing—51, 130, 143.

A special word must be said about the seeming self-righteousness of prayers for vindication like Psalm 26. The writer is not saying that he is entirely without sin, but that he is innocent of a particular accusation that has been made against him. In such cases (1 Kings 8 : 31) a man might be compelled to swear his innocence before the altar. From Psalm 26 : 6–7 we learn that the oath of innocence and prayer for vindication were accompanied by a ceremony of hand-washing and walking round the altar while singing a hymn.

7. *Individual songs of thanksgiving* are frequent in the Psalm-Book. Psalm 107 is particularly interesting in this connection, because it describes various deliverances for which men gave thanks. Evidently these were occasions when sacrifices were offered which the worshipper had vowed to God when he was in distress. "Praise is due to thee, O God, in Zion; and to thee shall vows be performed" (Psalm 65 : 1; see also 66 :

13–15 and Jonah 2). Evidently, too, this was done in the presence of the congregation; "I will pay my vows to the LORD in the presence of all his people, in the courts of the house of the LORD" (Psalm 116 : 18–19).

8. *Individual prayers of faith and trust in God* often are part of, or related to, entreaties for deliverance, as in 16, 25, 40. At other times they are independent— related to the prayers of thanksgiving, as in 23, 27, 121. With these we may take such meditations on the greatness and goodness of God as 8, 91 and 103. Psalm 1 reminds us of the Beatitudes in Matthew 5. Psalms 37 and 49 set forth the true wisdom concerning man's life here on earth, and in 73 the psalmist, considering life's contradictions, affirms that the God who has been his friend in this life will be his portion forever.

9. The *Psalms of approach to worship* express a similar attitude of faith and trust, and at the same time set out the obligations in belief and character which rest on those who would draw near to God. "Who shall ascend the hill of the LORD? And who shall stand in his holy place? He who has clean hands and a pure heart" (Psalm 24 : 3–4). Psalms 15, 84 and 122 may be compared with this. These Psalms speak of the individual's faith and his obligations, but they belong also to the common acknowledgment of God in congregational worship.

Thus, with many voices and in differing moods, the "sweet singers of Israel" uttered the prayers and praises which have been preserved for us in the Book of Psalms. The circumstances of our lives in this modern world differ from theirs, but our spiritual needs are much the same. It is for this reason that we so often find in the Psalms words which express what we most want to say to God.

CHAPTER THREE

HOW THE PSALM-BOOK CAME TO US

The Psalms have come down to us through two channels—through the Bible, and through the hymn-books and prayer-books of the Church. In the time of our Lord, the Psalm-Book as we find it in our Bibles had already been completed and accepted as sacred Scripture for two centuries or more. The Hebrew Bible which was read in the synagogues and which Jesus knew so well was known as "the Law of Moses, and the Prophets, and the Psalms" (Luke 24 : 44). In the third and second centuries B.C. this Bible was translated into Greek for the many Jews outside Palestine who were forgetting the Hebrew language. Since most of the early Christians were Greek-speaking, the Greek Old Testament became their first Bible; to it, as time went on, the books of the New Testament were added.

The Psalms came into the Christian Church, then, in a translation from the original Hebrew in which they had been written. Later they were again translated into Latin, and in this form served the undivided western Church for more than a thousand years. The Roman Catholic Church still uses the Psalms in Latin, while the old Greek translation continues to be used in Eastern Orthodox churches. Most versions of the Bible in English and other modern languages are translated from the original Hebrew in which the Psalms were first composed, and which was carefully copied by Jewish scribes for many centuries.

The second channel through which the Psalms have reached us is the service books of the Christian churches.

The first Christian congregations took over from the Jewish synagogues the practice of using the Psalms as hymns and prayers in worship. We hear of them singing "psalms and hymns and spiritual songs with thankfulness to God" (Colossians 3 : 16). Before long certain selected Psalms and Psalm verses were in regular use and were copied in service books. The Psalm-Book as a whole appeared as a separate booklet to be used in worship and in private devotions. In the monasteries the full one hundred and fifty Psalms were chanted once a week in the eight daily services, a constant round of prayer and praise. At one time candidates for ordination were expected to know all the Psalms by heart.

The daily services of Morning and Evening Prayer in the Prayer Book of the Anglican Communion are based on the monastic services, and provide for the reading of the whole Psalter once a month. The Prayer Book version of the Psalms in English differs a little from that in the English Bible because it is a sixteenth-century version made from the Latin Bible. This was retained in the Prayer Book because it had become so familiar, when the Authorized Version of 1611 was adopted for other parts of the Scripture used in the services. Still another form is that used in the Presbyterian and Reformed branches of Christendom, where the Psalms have been put into metrical verse for use as hymns.

It is interesting to compare the opening verses of the best loved of all the Psalms in the Authorized Version, and in the Prayer Book and metrical versions:

> The LORD is my shepherd; I shall not want.
> He maketh me to lie down in green pastures:
> he leadeth me beside the still waters. (*Authorized Version*)
>
> The LORD is my shepherd: therefore can I lack nothing.
> He shall feed me in a green pasture:
> and lead me forth beside the waters of comfort. (*Book of Common Prayer*)

The LORD's my shepherd, I'll not want.
He makes me down to lie
In pastures green; he leadeth me
The quiet waters by. (*Metrical Psalter*)

The Long Tradition of Praise in Israel

We have been speaking so far of the completed Psalm-Book which was taken over by the early Christians from the Jewish religion in which our Lord was brought up. But we have not fully answered the question as to how the Psalms came to us, until we have considered how they came to be written in the first place. In Chapter 2 we saw that many Psalms were composed for, or adapted to, the congregational and individual forms of worship in the temple, before and after the Exile of the Jews in Babylon. Yet this is only part of the story. Songs of praise to God were sung before Solomon's temple was built. We find also later poems of meditation and devotion which evidently were meant for private use and study, with no particular relation to community worship in temple or synagogue.

The Psalm-Book gathers together the fruits of a long and living tradition of religious poetry in Israel. We can trace its beginnings in the poetical blessings and curses which the Book of Genesis tells us were uttered by the patriarchs—Noah (9 : 25–27), Isaac (27 : 27–29, 39–40) and Jacob (48 : 15–16, 20; 49 : 2–27). For example:

May God give you of the dew of heaven,
  and of the richness of the earth,
  and plenty of grain and wine.
Let peoples serve you,
  and nations bow down to you . . .
Cursed be every one who curses you,
  and blessed be every one who blesses you!
(Genesis 27 : 28–29)

These early invocations of God's power find close

42

parallels in such Psalms as 35, 83, 128 and 137. The Blessing of Melchizedek in Genesis 14 : 19–20, a thanksgiving for victory over a king's enemies, recalls the latter part of Psalm 18.

Israel became a nation through the tremendous experiences of the Exodus from Egypt. The theme of God's mighty acts of revelation and deliverance at that time recurs in hymns of thanksgiving like Psalm 106, and in prayers of supplication like Psalm 80. If we turn to the story of the deliverance from the pursuing Egyptians at the Red Sea in Exodus 14 and 15, we hear Miriam and all the women sing a hymn of triumph:

> Sing to the LORD, for he has triumphed gloriously;
> the horse and his rider he has thrown into the sea.
> (Exod. 15:21)

The words of this ancient chorus provide the text for the Psalm in Exod. 15 : 1–18 known as "the Song of Moses and the people of Israel", which (as we can see from the reference to Solomon's temple in verse 17) is one of the temple Psalms dealing with the theme of the Exodus deliverance. The victory chant of women is referred to again in the time of the Philistine wars, when they danced and sang to the accompaniment of musical instruments:

> Saul has slain his thousands,
> And David his ten thousands. (1 Samuel 18 : 7)

In Deborah's song in Judges 5, a famous victory is celebrated in the manner of a ballad which is also a shout of praise (verse 31).

Another type of religious song in early Israel is described in 1 Samuel 10 : 5–6. A band of prophets is pictured as "prophesying" in a kind of marching song, to the accompaniment of musical instruments. This reminds us of the much later account in 1 Chronicles

25 : 1–8 of the arrangements for the musical services of the temple, where the clans of Asaph, Heman and Jeduthun were to "prophesy with lyres, with harps, and with cymbals . . . in thanksgiving and praise to the LORD". We have already noticed these names in the headings of certain Psalms, so that "to prophesy" here means "to speak the truth of God in hymns of praise".

When King David brought the Ark of God to Jerusalem, it was "with shouting, and with the sound of the horn" (2 Samuel 6 : 1–15). A similar procession in the later temple ceremonial is in the psalmist's mind when he says, "God (i.e. the ark of God) has gone up (i.e. to the temple hill) with a triumphant shout; the LORD with the sound of a trumpet" (Psalm 47 : 5). The "shout" was probably a short couplet repeated over and over like the triumph song of the women already referred to. In Psalm 18 (which is found also in slightly different form in 2 Samuel 22) we have the poetic expansion of such a shout:

> The LORD is my rock, and my fortress,
> My deliverer, in whom I take refuge,
> My shield, and the horn of my salvation.

The account in 1 Kings 8 of the dedication of Solomon's temple throws further light on the development of the Psalms. The king, in these early days, often took the place of the chief priest. Here Solomon utters a blessing upon the assembled congregation in words which are found also in Psalm 72 : 18 :

> Blessed be the LORD, the God of Israel.

Then follows a long prayer of dedication in which Solomon names the various situations in which a psalm of entreaty would be addressed to God in this house which he had built for His worship—the prayer for vindication of innocence (vss. 31–32, see Psalm 26); the

44

prayer for divine mercy on the occasion of national defeat by an enemy (vss. 33–34, see Psalm 44); the prayer for rain in time of drought (vss. 35–36, see Psalms 65 and 85); other prayers in different distresses (vss. 37–40, see Psalm 69); prayer before battle (vss. 44–45, see Psalm 20).

At royal coronations, a trumpet was blown and the people clapped their hands, shouting "Long live the king!" (1 Kings 1 : 39; 2 Kings 11 : 12). This sentence recurs in Psalm 72 : 15, a Psalm which seems to have been used as a coronation ode. Such an ode was composed for the special occasion, and probably was chanted by a prophet in the course of the ceremonies in the temple. It would not normally be used in regular congregational worship.

In the books of the prophets of the eighth and seventh centuries there are several references to singing, in the worship of the sanctuaries. Amos 5 : 23 speaks of "the noise of your songs, and the melody of your harps" at the festivals of sacrifice. In Amos 8 : 3 there is a further reference to "the songs of the temple" which will be turned into wailing on the day of God's judgment. Isaiah 30 : 29 says:

> You shall have a song, as in the night
> When a holy feast is kept. (cf. Psalm 134 : 1)

Jeremiah speaks of "the voices of those who sing, as they bring thankofferings to the house of the LORD":

> Give thanks to the LORD of hosts,
>   for the LORD is good,
>   for his mercy endures forever! (Jer. 33 : 11)

The temple chants were stilled for a time when, in 586 B.C., Jerusalem was captured by the Babylonians and the temple was burned. Large numbers of the Jewish people were carried away into exile. After some years had passed, one of them pictured the sadness and homesickness of the strangers in a strange land in the words of a poem which has become Psalm 137:

> By the rivers of Babylon,
>   there we sat down and wept,
> When we remembered Zion . . .
> For there our captors required of us songs,
>   and our tormentors, mirth, saying—
> "Sing us one of the songs of Zion".

In the year 538 B.C., Cyrus the Persian king overthrew Babylon, and permitted the exiled Jews to return to Palestine and rebuild their ruined temple. Another psalmist rejoices in the memory of that happy time:

> When the LORD restored the fortunes of Zion,
> We were like those who dream.
> Then our mouth was filled with laughter,
> And our tongue with the shout of joy. (Psalm 126 : 1–2)

The Hebrew word which here is translated "shout of joy" is used in Psalm 107 : 22 of the Psalm of thanksgiving which accompanied the temple sacrifice of the thankoffering. In fact, Psalm 107 is itself such a Psalm. We are told in Ezra 3 : 10–13 that, when the foundation was laid for the rebuilding of the temple, the priests and Levites sang the response which is familiar from many Psalms:

> Give thanks to the LORD, for he is good,
> For his mercy endures forever,

. . . and all the people shouted with a great shout.

In this period after the Babylonian Exile, old Psalms were collected and new Psalms composed for use by the temple choirs and orchestras which traced their history back to the days of David (1 Chronicles 15 : 16–16 : 42). We cannot always be sure whether a Psalm was composed originally for worship in the temple of Jerusalem. It may have come from one of the other sanctuaries of the Lord, like Bethel, where Jacob worshipped

46

and Amos prophesied, or from Shiloh, where Eli was priest. This is a question which is interesting as we study the history behind the Bible, but it does not matter greatly when we use the Psalms in worship. When we sing Christian hymns, it does not make any difference to us whether they were written by a Roman Catholic poet many centuries ago, or by a Protestant in recent years. What matters is that we can make their words our own when we sing praise to God.

Psalms of the People of God

Every Psalm was written in the first place by some individual poet, and expresses what his religious experience meant to him. This is true, even though we must allow for the fact that sometimes a Psalm or hymn was slightly altered by the later collectors who put it into their book, just as the editors of hymn-books to-day sometimes modify the text of the hymns which they print. But the psalmists were not merely solitary worshippers. In many cases they were spokesmen for the fellowship to which they belonged, the ancient Jewish church, the Chosen People of God.

The writers speak from experience. We have still to ask if they are speaking as individuals for themselves, or on behalf of a worshipping congregation. Or, are many speaking the same words in unison? as when we sing:

> *I* heard the voice of Jesus say,
> Come unto me, and rest.

One thing which is quite certain is that the Psalm-Book contains many prayers for use by individuals as well as many others for congregational use. The temple ritual itself provided for the payment of vows in individual acts of worship (1 Samuel 1 : 3–2 : 10; Acts 21 : 23–26). People went there by themselves at other times to pray (1 Kings 8 : 41–42; Luke 18 : 10), and certainly individuals said their prayers at home and elsewhere (Daniel 6 : 10; Matt. 6 : 6). Many prayers such as Psalms 13, 42–43 and 51 are intensely personal. The prayer for vindication against unjust accusations in Psalm 26, and the prayer accompanying the sacrifice in payment of a vow in Psalm 116, are evidently spoken by each man on his own account.

On the other hand, although Psalm 129 is written like these in the first person singular, it includes the notation that it is to be recited by "Israel", that is, by the assembled congregation. The "me" is "Israel", the worshipping congregation.

> Sorely have they afflicted me from my youth,
>   (let Israel say)
> Sorely have they afflicted me from my youth,
> Yet they have not prevailed against me.

In Psalm 60 : 9 we read:

> Who will bring me to the fortified city?

The context makes it clear that the writer has in mind the king and the armies of Israel.

The way in which the writer speaks for himself and also for his people, is illustrated by those passages where he begins by saying "I" and goes on to say "we". In Psalm 123 : 1–2 we find:

> To thee *I* lift up my eyes . . .
> As the eyes of servants look to the hand of their master . . .
> So *our* eyes look to the LORD our God.

Many Psalms use "we" only (see Psalms 44, 48, 67). In Psalm 135

> . . . the servants of the LORD,
> who stand in the house of the LORD

praise the Lord, saying:

> I know that the LORD is great.

48

Many of the Psalms, therefore, express the prayers and praises of the Church of Israel. Not only so, but they speak out of the community's experience of God's dealings with them as His people. Their need was a common need. Theirs was a shared faith and a shared hope in the Lord. These Psalms have come down from the Church of the Old Covenant to the Church of the New Covenant. But the Church of the Old Covenant is not just like the Church of the New. Israel was also a *nation* which was in many ways like other nations. It had its own national life and history. The salvation of which many psalmists speak was God's deliverance of His people in this world, and of individuals chiefly as members of the community. A second difference is that God had not yet visited and redeemed His people through the life, the death and the resurrection of Jesus Christ our Lord. The praise and prayers of the Old Covenant had not yet been transformed by the spirit and power of the New. When we use the national Psalms in Christian worship, we must interpret them in the light of the universal Gospel of Jesus Christ.

Nevertheless, as we shall see in the next chapter, the Psalms can indeed *become* Christian praise when they are used in that fuller light. Their God is the same God who sent the prophets to call men to Himself, and who, last of all, sent His Son. They come from an earlier time and stage of the revelation of which Jesus Christ was both the climax and a new beginning. They are like the first light of morning which grows ever brighter until at last the sun has risen and the new day begins.

The Differing Notes of Worship

The Psalms strike various notes. We observe first, hymns of sheer praise which rejoice in the greatness and goodness of God. Ten of these, including the last five in the collection, are built on the Hebrew words "Halleluʹ-jah" ("Praise the LORD!"), a frequent shout expressing exultant religious joy. It is the Lord—

> Who made heaven and earth,
> The sea, and all that is in them,
> Who keeps faith for ever,
> Who secures justice for the oppressed,
> Who gives food to the hungry. (Psalm 146 : 6–7)

Other hymns begin, like the *Venite* (Psalm 95; see also Psalm 100), with a similar summons to sing the Lord's praises, not only for His greatness and power, but in particular because He has drawn near to us in mercy:

> We are his people, and the sheep of his pasture. (Psalm 100 : 3)

Still other Psalms dwell on the thought of the divine sovereignty and the certainty that God's righteousness will triumph:

> He is coming to judge the earth;
> He will judge the world with righteousness,
> And peoples with his truth. (Psalm 96 : 13)

Closely related to these poems are the hymns of thanksgiving for God's "mighty acts" in the past, His creation of the world and His choice and deliverance of His people. These are the grounds of Israel's faith:

> Praise is due to thee, O God, in Zion . . .
> By dread deeds thou dost answer us righteously,
> O God of our salvation . . .
> Who art the hope of all the ends of the earth . . .
> Who by thy strength hast established the mountains. (Psalm
>   65 : 1, 5, 6)

> In Judah is God known,
> His name is great in Israel . . .
> Glorious art thou,
> More majestic than the everlasting mountains . . .
> At thy rebuke, O God of Jacob,
> Both rider and horse lay stunned. (Psalm 76 : 1, 4, 6)

50

(The poet is referring here to the overthrow of Pharaoh's
army at the Red Sea; see Exodus 15 : 1.)

> Moses and Aaron were among his priests,
> Samuel also was among those who called on his name,
> They cried to the LORD, and he answered them.
>
> (Psalm 99 : 6)
>
> Bless the LORD, O my soul,
> And forget not all his benefits. (Psalm 103 : 2)

The dominant note of these hymns of faith and thanksgiving is well expressed in Psalm 126 : 3—

> The LORD has done great things for us;
> So we rejoice.

Among the more general hymns of praise for the gift
of life and salvation, there are some which seem to refer
to particular blessings and deliverances. Psalm 124
gives God the glory for His merciful deliverance in time
of war:

> If it had not been the LORD who was on our side,
> When men rose up against us,
> Then they would have swallowed us up alive.
>
> (Psalm 124 : 2–3)

The mood of the poets is different in the many
prayers of God's people uttered in times of trial. Sometimes they feel that faith is fighting a losing battle:

> Help, LORD, for there is no longer any one that is godly;
> For the faithful have vanished from among the sons of men.
>
> (Psalm 12 : 1)

Injustice is rampant, and arrogant wickedness seems
to be in control:

> Rise up, O judge of the earth;
> Render to the proud their deserts . . .
> They pour out their arrogant words . . .
> They crush thy people, O LORD. (Psalm 94 : 2, 4, 5)

Why does God not act? Why is He silent? Is it because He is angry with His people? Has He abandoned them altogether? The writer of Psalm 44 : 23 even suggests that God appears to be asleep, or indifferent to Israel's affliction; so, "Rouse thyself! Why sleepest thou, O Lord? Awake!"

> Why dost thou stand far off, O LORD?
> Why dost thou hide thyself in times of trouble?
> (Psalm 10 : 1)
> O God, do not keep silence! (Psalm 83 : 1)
> Wilt thou be angry with us for ever? (Psalm 85 : 5)

Some Psalms seem to have been composed for use at particular religious festivals, just as we have hymns especially suited to the festivals of the Christian year.

> Raise a song, sound the timbrel . . .
> Blow the trumpet at the new moon, (and)
> At the full moon for our festival.
> (Psalm 81 : 2–3; see Isaiah 1 : 13)

The reference in verse 5 of this Psalm to the Lord's going out "over the land of Egypt" indicates that this is a song for the annual *Passover* celebration. Another such is Psalm 135. For the Festival of Harvest, Psalms 65 and 67 would be appropriate:

> Thou visitest the earth and dost water it . . .
> Thou crownest the year with thy bounty. (Psalm 65 : 9, 11)

At the *New Year's festival* the worshippers sang a "new song" of allegiance to the Lord, as the supreme and victorious king whose righteous judgments determine the destinies of all men and nations.

> O sing to the LORD a new song . . .
> For great is the LORD, and greatly to be praised;
> He is to be feared above all gods . . .
> Say among the nations, "The LORD is King",
> He has established the world, it shall not be moved,
> He will judge the people with equity. (Psalm 96 : 1, 4, 10)

One further group of Psalms for use on public occasions is related to events in the national life of the community, rather than to the regular worship. We recall again that the people of God under the Old Covenant were also a nation among other nations. Even when the monarchy came to an end and the high priest replaced the king as head of the community, Israel thought of herself as a chosen race with a national history. Certain of the Psalms reflect, as we have remarked before, this national aspect of the community's experience, especially the distinctive role of the king.

Psalm 45, in fact, is not a prayer or hymn to God at all, but a poem addressed to the reigning king and his bride on the occasion of their wedding. It is included among the Psalms because the king was thought of as not an ordinary person, but one chosen and anointed for his sacred office as head of God's people and chief priest of the nation. The Hebrew word for "anointed" is *Messiah*, and this is how the words of the Psalm came to be applied in Hebrews 1 to Jesus, the true Messiah.

It is when we turn to such compositions as Psalms 46 and 48 that we see at its best the faith of Israel as related to a crisis in the national life. No matter what disaster comes, faith will not yield to fear.

> God is for us a refuge and strength,
> A really present help in trouble;
> Therefore we will not fear
> Though the earth should change. (Psalm 46 : 1–2)

In both of these Psalms the city of Zion, ancient and historic, the place of pilgrimage and worship, has become a symbol of the presence of God in the midst of His people. The people repeat in chorus their confident faith in the help of the God of the heavenly hosts, who is also the God of their ancestor Jacob and their God. Their national life rests on deep and strong foundations, and on these they rely when "waters roar and foam". A nation's character shows itself in times of conflict and trial, when all the world can see what its people live by and are willing to die for. Israel became a people under the leadership of God's prophet Moses. Though she often departed from His ways, Israel knew what God had done for her, and that in Him alone was her security, welfare, and hope for the future.

> The LORD of hosts is with us,
> The God of Jacob is our fortress. (Psalm 46 : 7)

Psalms of the Individual Believer

The Psalms which have come to us out of the personal religious experiences of individuals perhaps speak to our hearts more directly than do those which have come out of community experiences of ancient Israel. Even though these prayers and praises have been passed on to us by men who lived so long ago and so far away, they voice in an incomparable way the cry of the soul to the living God. Indeed, one of their most striking characteristics is their passionate earnestness. These are not the conventional prayers of the lips. They speak from the depths of man's being to Him who hears and answers prayer, and whose answer is the life of man's spirit.

The dominant note of the prayers of the individual in the Psalm-Book is entreaty or supplication. The writers speak of their utter helplessness, and need of God's aid and salvation. Sometimes it is because they are seriously ill and in danger of death, beyond which, for them, was no hope of blessed immortality. "The dead praise not the LORD, nor do any that go down into silence" (Psalm 115 : 17). So—

> O LORD, save my life. (Psalm 6 : 4)
> My strength is dried up like a potsherd,
> And my tongue cleaves to my jaws. (Psalm 22 : 15)

Frequently the writer speaks of being in trouble through the vindictiveness of personal enemies, or of being forsaken by his friends:

> All who hate me whisper together about me . . .
> Even my close friend whom I trusted . . .
> Has lifted up his heel against me. (Psalm 41 : 7, 9)

Others are falsely accused of wrongdoing, and are bitter under a sense of injustice:

> False witnesses have risen up against me. (Psalm 27 : 12)
> What I did not steal, must I now restore? (Psalm 69 : 4)

The mockery which pours scorn on the psalmists' faith is among their greatest trials:

> My tears have been my food day and night,
> While men say to me continually,
> Where is your God? (Psalm 42 : 3)

They are in an agony of perplexity when prayer goes unanswered:

> My God, my God, why hast thou forsaken me? (Psalm 22 : 1)

—words which Jesus echoed from the Cross. The eternal God is their only refuge and hope (Psalm 22 : 19).

Indeed it is noteworthy that what these ancient saints desired above all from God was the assurance of His presence and concern, to vindicate the right and to restore them to the joy of conscious fellowship with Him. Their prayer is not for His gifts, but for Himself.

> I stretch out my hands to thee;
> My soul thirsts for thee like a parched land. (Psalm 143 : 6)

They appeal to His mercy, His justice and His faithfulness (Psalm 86 : 15). They cast themselves upon the divine protection (Psalm 71 : 1). While imploring vindication from unjust accusations (Psalm 26), they are ready to be tested and to accept punishment when it is deserved (Psalm 7 : 3–5). Psalm 141 might have been written from the text "Lead us not into temptation".

The psalmists fully recognize the moral conditions, under which alone prevailing prayer can be uttered. They confess their own sin and unworthiness, and humbly cast themselves on God's mercy. They acknowledge their obligation to "what God requires". They know that the sacrifice which really matters to God is the surrender of pride and the dedication of the will. Their faith creates hope, as they wait in eager expectation for the answer of the God in whom they trust.

> O LORD, pardon my guilt, for it is great. (Psalm 25 : 11)
> Create in me a clean heart, O God. . . .
> The sacrifice acceptable to God is a broken spirit,
> A broken and contrite heart,
> O God, thou wilt not despise. (Psalm 51 : 10–17)
> I wait for the LORD, my soul waits,
> And in his word I hope. (Psalm 130 : 5)
> My soul thirsts for God, for the living God. (Psalm 42 : 2)

Prayers of thanksgiving, affirmations of faith, and meditations on the greatness of God and the wonder of His revelation, are the principal types of individual utterances remaining to be considered. It is a striking fact that there are no prayers of intercession; it is from Christ Himself that we have learned to pray for one another.

The thanksgivings are both general and specific.

> Give thanks to his holy name,
> For his anger is but for a moment,
> While his favour is for a lifetime. (Psalm 30 : 4–5)
> O give thanks to the LORD, for he is good,
> For his lovingkindness endures for ever. (Psalm 136 : 1)

Some of the prayers of entreaty, such as Psalms 54 and 69, conclude with a burst of praise for the answer which has been given. Other Psalms are devoted wholly to gratitude for the response which the worshipper has found to his cry of need:

> I give thee thanks, O LORD, with my whole heart . . .
> On the day that I called, thou didst answer me.
>
> (Psalm 138 : 1, 3)

The answer that matters most is the gift of abundant life in God's realized presence:

> Thou dost show me the path of life,
> In thy presence is fulness of joy. (Psalm 16 : 11)

The affirmations of faith are not abstract but intensely personal in their reasons. Here is the living tradition which links past and present in the "communion of saints":

> In thee our fathers trusted,
> They trusted, and thou didst deliver them. (Psalm 22 : 4)

Psalm 23 looks back on the overflowing goodness of the divine companionship and care, in dark days as well as in bright. Psalm 91 shows that the believer who lives consciously "in the shadow of the Almighty" finds a lifelong shelter from crippling fear in times of danger. In Psalm 125 a pilgrim sees in the encircling hills a token of God's sleepless care. Psalm 73 tells how faith was tried:

> My steps had well nigh slipped,
> For I was envious of the arrogant . . .
> (thinking)
> All for nothing have I kept my heart clean. (vss. 2, 3, 13)

It was in the renewed experience of worship that understanding came:

> Thou hast put them in slippery places . . .
> How they can be destroyed in a moment! . . .
> But I am continually with thee . . .
> And there is nothing upon earth that I desire besides thee.
>
> (vss. 18, 19, 23, 25)

One of the supreme expressions of the assurance of knowing and being known by God is found in Psalm 139:

> O LORD, thou hast searched me and known me . . .
> Thou dost beset me behind and before,
> And layest thine hand upon me . . .
> Whither could I go from thy Spirit?
> Or whither could I flee from thy presence? . . .
> Search me, O God, and know my heart . . .
> And lead me in the way everlasting. (vss. 1, 5, 7, 23–24)

Some of the greatest of the Psalms are meditations on God and His revelation which rise on wings of faith to adoring praise.

> O taste and see that the LORD is good! (Psalm 34 : 8)
> The LORD is my light and my salvation;
> Whom shall I fear? (Psalm 27 : 1)
> The LORD God is a sun and shield . . .
> O LORD of hosts, happy is the man who trusts in thee!
> (Psalm 84 : 11, 12)

> LORD, thou hast been our dwelling place in all generations;
> Before the mountains were brought forth,
> Or ever thou hadst formed the broad earth,
> From everlasting to everlasting thou art God.
> (Psalm 90 : 1–2)

In such passages as these we find the most important answer to the question which forms the title of this chapter. In the providence of the God and Father of our Lord Jesus Christ, these utterances of a living faith have been preserved from ancient times that they might help to kindle a like faith in us. Through all the centuries they have been constantly on the lips of countless men and women like ourselves. They teach us how to pray, as our Lord taught His disciples. He Himself used these words to speak to His Father in heaven. The Psalm-Book of Israel has become one of the most precious parts of Christian Scripture.

CHAPTER FOUR

JEWISH PSALMS IN THE CHRISTIAN'S BIBLE

Something has been said already in the Introduction about the reasons for which Christians have always treasured the Psalms. They provide for us, more than any other part of the Bible, the language of praise and prayer. They provide for the needs of the individual as well as of the worshipping congregation. Their appeal is to all sorts and conditions of men. The fact that they are so widely used throughout all Christian churches to-day, and have been so used for many centuries, shows how close the worship of ancient Israel, at its best, approached to the ideal of worship "in spirit and in truth".

Yet the other fact remains, too, that the Psalms have been inherited by us from the pre-Christian worship of temple and synagogue. They speak in the language of the ancient time and of the different circumstances in which they were written. They represent an earlier stage of revelation and faith. Of necessity, therefore, they fall short at many points of the fulness of the Christian understanding of God's ways, and of the joyous certainty of New Testament faith. As Christians we must read their words in a new way, because in Christ all things are become new.

The Jewish origin of the Psalms, moreover, makes some difficulties for the Christian when he repeats their words in his worship of God. He comes across words and figures of speech which convey no clear meaning, because they reflect conditions of life and ideas which belong to that far-off day in a distant land. He may find himself repeating words which imply that he is present in the temple of Solomon, where the priests were "offering repeatedly the same sacrifices which can never take away sin" (Hebrews 10 : 11). Other passages which refer to particular circumstances in the national life of Israel seem out of place in the universal worship of the Church. Above all, there are certain religious beliefs and ideas of right and wrong, which we cannot wholly subscribe to, since Christ's coming has brought a more perfect apprehension of the truth of God.

As we can see from the Gospels, our Lord knew the Psalms well, and nourished His own spiritual life from them. But He used them with discrimination, and not literally like the scribes. In the same way His modern disciples must learn to distinguish between the letter and the spirit, between the temporary and the permanent, between a partial understanding of God's truth with its yearning for fuller knowledge, and the answer to that yearning which came with Jesus Christ. It will help us to do this if we observe some of the marks which remain on the Psalms from that earlier stage of divine revelation.

Hebrew Forms of Expression

When a book is translated from one language into another, the translators often have difficulty in making the exact meaning of it clear. This is because words and expressions have different associations in the life and literature of different societies. Peculiar forms of expression, which would be familiar to the original readers, may be meaningless or may convey a quite mistaken impression when translated literally. There are examples of this in the Psalms, of which the following are samples:

Do not lift up your horn on high. (Psalm 75 : 5)

This means—"Do not be proud and stubborn". The figure is taken from the attitude of the wild ox, which stubbornly held its horns high and refused to have a yoke put on its neck (see Psalm 92 : 10). In countries where the wild ox is never seen, this expression has to be explained.

Again, in Psalm 42 : 2 we read:

When shall I come and behold the face of God?

The older translations turned this round so that it read: "When shall I come and appear before God?", because of the saying that no one could see God's face and live (Exodus 33 : 20). But this was needlessly scrupulous, for the story of Joseph and his brothers in Genesis 43 : 3 makes it clear that "to see one's face" was simply an expression for "to be admitted to one's presence" (the presence of some great person).

A third example is an oft quoted mistranslation:

O worship the LORD in the beauty of holiness! ((Psalm 96 : 9)

The word translated "beauty" means rather "adornment", so that the reference is to the *sacred adornment* of worshippers (see 2 Chronicles 20 : 21; Ezekiel 44 : 17–19).

In other passages we find metaphors used which are strange to us because they are drawn from unfamiliar customs or experiences. "The LORD is my chosen portion and my cup" (Psalm 16 : 5) refers to the passing of a cup to a guest. We recall the words of Jesus: "Shall I not drink the cup which the Father has given me?" (John 18 : 11). Again, "Thou anointest my head with oil" (Psalm 23 : 5) pictures a courtesy paid to a guest.

"I am like a green olive tree in the house of God" (Psalm 52 : 8) is a metaphor meant to suggest life and fruitfulness in a dry and stony land; it loses some of its force for readers who live where trees are abundant.

The Language of Temple Ritual

Many of the Psalms originated as hymns, prayers, vows, benedictions and other ritual words which accompanied the sacrifices, processions and other ceremonial acts of temple worship. In such Psalms as 24, 68 and 118 the reference to worship ceremonies is unmistakable. Others of the prayers and hymns have been modified for use in the synagogue, where no animals were slain at a smoking altar. In the later period of Jewish worship, prayer had been substituted for the actual offerings prescribed in the Law of Moses. Even at the temple itself prophetic voices declared that what God wants most from His servants is the devotion of their hearts, rather than the gifts they bring.

> Burnt offering and sin offering thou hast not required;
> Then I said, See, I come . . .
> I delight to do thy will, O my God. (Psalm 40 : 6–8)

And again,

> Thou delightest not in a burnt offering;
> The sacrifices of God are a broken spirit;
> A broken and contrite heart, O God,
> Thou wilt not despise. (Psalm 51 : 16–17)

The Christian knows that "it is impossible that the blood of bulls and goats should take away sins", and that Christ "has appeared once for all at the end of the age to put away sin by the sacrifice of himself" (Hebrews 10 : 4; 9 : 26). When, therefore, in our reading or recitation of the Psalms we come upon words which were originally used in sacrificial rites, we can share the devotion they were intended to express without taking the language literally. For example—we do not wash our hands to proclaim our innocence as we walk round an altar in ceremonial procession (see Psalm 26 : 6). Yet we *can* use these words to express our purpose to turn from our wickedness and live. When we pray for inner cleansing, quoting Psalm 51 : 7, we are not sprinkled with a sprig of the *hyssop* bush as the ancient worshippers were, but we share their profound sense of the need for purity. We may repeat the vow of burnt offerings from Psalm 66 : 13–15, but for us it is a simple pledge of dedication to the will and to the service of God.

We do not, like the Israelites, celebrate a religious festival at the New Moon, though we can still "sing aloud to God our strength" in a song of praise preserved from their service on that occasion (Psalm 81 : 1, 3). The "cup of salvation" of Psalm 116 : 13 was a goblet from which a thankoffering of wine was poured out in gratitude for recovery from illness. It has a new meaning for us—the communion cup which is the symbol of Christ's blood poured out for many for the remission of sins. The words are the same, but their meaning has changed because they have acquired new and richer associations.

Unchristian Beliefs and Attitudes

Certain beliefs expressed or implied in some places in the Psalms are less than Christian, and as we repeat them we must recognize and allow for the fact that a truer revelation has now been given in Christ.

This is evident, for instance, in the way the psalmists think and speak of death. These ancient saints lived too soon to be able to share the faith of Christ's resurrection. Though some, greatly daring, hope that their fellowship with God will not be interrupted by physical death (see Psalm 73 : 23–26), others have no such consolation:

63

> In death there is no remembrance of thee;
> In the grave, who can give thee praise? (Psalm 6 : 5)
> The dead praise not the LORD,
> Nor do any that go down into silence. (Psalm 115 : 17)

These men thought also that every illness was a sign of God's displeasure, and hence that it could be cured if the sins were to be acknowledged and forgiven.

> There is no soundness in my flesh,
> Because of thy indignation,
> There is no health in my bones
> Because of my sin. (Psalm 38 : 3)

We do indeed believe that there is a broad connection between man's alienation from God and the physical illnesses which afflict mankind. But we know also that many who are physically well are spiritually sick, and conversely, that even the most saintly can suffer grievous illness. When Psalm 112 declares that the man who fears the Lord will be rewarded with prosperity and success, the writer is describing an ideal case rather than laying down a universal rule. Indeed, to the writer of Psalm 73 the health and prosperity of the wicked present an agonizing problem. He is able to solve the problem only on the spiritual plane, when, as he meditates in the temple, he learns to see the situation in the light of God's countenance, and to recognize that the thing that really matters is not earthly prosperity but unbroken fellowship with God.

Another point at which some at least of the Psalm writers come short of Christian belief is their attitude to the gods worshipped by other peoples. Although the First Commandment is—"Thou shalt have no other gods before me" (or, "in addition to me"), this did not settle the question whether other gods existed and had real power. Some of the psalmists speak as if the other gods existed, but that the Lord was greater than they:

> Before the gods I sing thy praise. (Psalm 138 : 1)
> There is none like thee among the gods, O Lord.
> (Psalm 86 : 8)

Psalm 82 pictures the Lord as summoning the lesser gods to the heavenly bar of judgment, where they are accused, in turn, of having judged human beings on earth unjustly and favoured the wicked. What this means is that gods who do injustice are false gods; they are unworthy to be worshipped, and therefore they are not real gods at all.

> The LORD . . . is to be feared above all gods,
> For all the gods of the peoples are idols;
> But the LORD made the heavens. (Psalm 96 : 4–5)

These gods are images only; there is no real divinity in them; but the heavens declare the power and wisdom of their Creator. In Psalm 115 : 3–8 the same contrast is made between man-made idols which cannot speak or see or hear or do anything at all, and the power and presence of the one living and true God.

A difficulty of somewhat different sort arises when the psalmists speak of God as if He had human form (though with wings like a bird). He rides on a cherub as men ride on a war horse (Psalm 18 : 10), and shoots His arrows like a bowman (Psalm 38 : 2). At other times He is seated on a heavenly throne, and laughs at earthly rulers who plot against Him and His Messiah (Psalm 2 : 4). These ways of speaking of God are not to be taken literally; they are figures of speech. What they mean is simply this—that God is personal. The only other beings with whom we can enter into personal relationships are human, and so it is only natural to speak to, and of, the Divine Person in much the same way. When

Genesis 1 : 27 says that "God created man in his own image", this means that there is a similarity between God and man which makes it possible for God to reveal Himself to man, and for man to speak to God.

Another difference between the language and spirit of the Gospel and that of some Psalms is seen in the vindictiveness which is so alien to our Lord's teaching that we must love our enemies and return good for evil.

> The righteous will rejoice when he sees vengeance,
> He will bathe his feet in the blood of the wicked.
>
> (Psalm 58 : 10)
>
> Raise me up, that I may requite them. (Psalm 41 : 10)

The most dreadful example of all is Psalm 137 : 9—

> Happy shall he be, who takes your little ones,
> And dashes them against the rock.

Here we see the difference which the coming of Christ has made. It is not enough to condemn the ancient Jews who felt and said these things. We must try to understand why they did so. To begin with, we must make some allowance for their way of emphasizing a thought by expressing it in an exaggerated and extravagant way. For example, when the poet wishes to express the thought of God's power which is seen in the shaking of the mountains in an earthquake, he says—

> He makes Lebanon to skip like a calf. (Psalm 29 : 6)

Everyone can see that this is a figure of speech, not to be taken literally.

The bitter cries for vengeance are expressed in this vehement way. Since these men did not know of judgment after death, they felt that God's justice must be vindicated here and now. They thought that this meant that the wicked must feel suffering like that which they had inflicted on others. Thus their words are more than a cry for personal revenge; they are also a plea that God would judge between right and wrong. The speakers had not yet learned that such things must be left to the goodness and wisdom of God, and, for themselves, to "repay no one evil for evil . . . but overcome evil with good" (Romans 12 : 17–21).

We have also to remember that they did not distinguish between the sin and the sinner, or understand that God would condemn sin, yet seek to win back the one who had committed it. Still less did they understand that we ourselves cannot expect God's forgiveness if we are unwilling to forgive those who trespass against us. Cruelty and arrogance were identified with cruel and arrogant men. Prayers for vengeance on such men were primarily prayers that these sins should not go unpunished.

Royal and Nationalistic Psalms

In ancient Israel there was no separation of Church and State. The religious community itself—the Chosen People—became for centuries a nation like other nations. The king who led them in battle and who administered justice like a judge, was, as we have seen, anointed like a priest and sometimes officiated at the altar. He prayed to God to support the national cause against the nation's enemies (see 1 Kings 1 : 39; 3 : 16–28; 8 : 44–45, 62–64; 22 : 29–38).

Certain of the Psalms, in consequence, strike a note which seems more political than religious. Psalm 20, for example, represents king and people as offering sacrifice and beseeching divine aid on the eve of battle. Psalm 60 begins with a supplication to God because of a defeat in war; a prophetic oracle follows in verses 6–8 in which the Lord is pictured as Israel's battle-champion.

Such a nationalist conception of a warrior god is unworthy of the Prince of Peace. Again, Psalm 48 : 4–7 celebrates a storm in which an enemy fleet has been destroyed. Psalm 83 prays for aid against a threatening alliance.

To-day the Christian Church is established in all lands. We join with our brothers to praise in many languages the one God and Father of us all. He is the King of Kings. We should, and do, pray to Him for the people to which we belong and the nation to which we owe loyalty as citizens. But when we repeat these ancient Psalms with nationalist associations, we must be careful not to identify too lightly our nation's cause with God's. It is God's cause to which we as Christians are committed, His perpetual warfare against evil. We must seek to have our nation committed to God's righteousness, and remember how much easier it is to see evil in our enemies than in ourselves.

The Jews believed not only that they were the Chosen People of God, but also that David and his descendants had been divinely chosen to rule over them.

> Of old thou didst speak in a vision . . .
> I have exalted one chosen from the people,
> I have found David my servant,
> With my holy oil I have anointed him,
> I have sworn to David my servant:
> I will establish your descendants for ever.
>
> (Psalm 89 : 19–20, 3–4)

In Psalm 2 the king is called the Lord's "anointed" (or, to use the Hebrew word, "Messiah"). In verse 7 he is called also God's "son", and the Lord declares the relationship formally:

> This day I have begotten you.

In another Psalm the priestly office of the king is affirmed:

> You are a perpetual priest,
> According to the order of Melchizedek. (Psalm 110 : 4)

When the Jewish kingdom had come to its end with the destruction of Jerusalem by the Babylonians in 586 B.C., the Jews for centuries were ruled by foreign empires. Yet their faith in the divine choice of the dynasty of David persisted. They believed that in His own good time God would send an "anointed king" or "Messiah" who would restore the kingdom to Israel, and who would be a more than human person. Thus it came about that words originally spoken of the Davidic kings before the destruction of Jerusalem and the Babylonian Exile, were now applied in their thinking to this God-sent "Messiah" of the future.

> May he have dominion from sea to sea,
> And from the River (Euphrates) to the ends of the earth.
> (Psalm 72 : 8)
>
> I will make him the first-born,
> The highest of the kings of the earth. (Psalm 89 : 27)
> The LORD says to my lord (the king):
> Sit at my right hand,
> Until I make your enemies your footstool. (Psalm 110 : 1)

What the true "Messiah-king" should be like had been declared by the prophets:

> The Spirit of the LORD shall rest upon him,
> The spirit of wisdom and understanding,
> The spirit of counsel and might,
> The spirit of knowledge and the fear of the LORD.
> (Isaiah 11 : 2)
>
> See, your king comes to you;
> Triumphant and victorious,
> Humble, riding on an ass. (Zechariah 9 : 9)

The kings of David's line had always fallen short of the ideal. Only in Jesus Christ was the perfect pattern realized. Thus the words of the prophets found their fulfilment in Him. When He came to John to be baptized He saw in a vision the heavens open, and He heard a voice, saying: "Thou art my son—the beloved, with whom I am well pleased" (Mark 1 : 11). The opening words are from Psalm 2 : 7, the Psalm of the anointed king who is acknowledged and commissioned by the King of Heaven. The remainder is a quotation from Isaiah 42 : 1, the prophecy of the missionary Servant of the Lord who suffered for the sins of many.

God's call thus came to our Lord expressed in the very words of ancient Scripture which He knew and loved. He was to be a "King-Messiah", but also a "Servant-Messiah" who was to be wounded for our transgressions. He refused the temptation to rule over the kingdoms of this world in earthly glory, for His "dominion from sea to sea" was to be in the hearts of men. He was more than all the prophets and psalmists had dreamed. Thus the titles and praise which originally had been addressed to Jewish anointed kings and of which they had proved unworthy, were at last applied with truth to Jesus; it is with the thought of Him in our minds that we can rightly sing these ancient and prophetic words.

CHAPTER FIVE

THE PSALMS AS CHRISTIAN SCRIPTURE

We have been seeking to understand the Psalms in the light of their origins in pre-Christian Jewish worship. This is important, but it is only a step toward something even more important—an understanding of the value and meaning of the Psalms as part of God's word. For in this modern age these ancient writings tell us of the One Living and True God, of the majesty of His power, the sureness of His justice, and the nearness of His everlasting mercy. The Psalms, indeed, do more than speak to us *about* God, His will, His judgment and His salvation. Through them God Himself still speaks to our hearts and minds, calling us to believe and to obey.

The men who wrote the Psalms lived before Christ came, but their faith and hope were in the same God who is *our* God, the God and Father of Jesus Christ our Lord. Thus what they wrote and prayed and sang has become Christian Scripture, part and parcel of the one revelation of the One God who spoke of old to our fathers by the prophets, and in later days had spoken to us by His Son. As we read the Psalms we realize that the God who speaks there and to whom the psalmists speak is the God we Christians worship. Sometimes clearly and sometimes more dimly the psalmists understood what God was teaching them. They have passed on to us the testimony of their faith and their knowledge of God. Sometimes they said more than they themselves fully understood, so that a Christian coming to the Psalms finds there anticipations of the fuller revelation

71

which was to come in Christ. "Blessed are they who have not seen and yet have believed".

The peculiar value of the Psalm-Book within the Bible is that it not only conveys God's Word to us but also assists us in addressing our prayers and praise to Him. In these sacred poems religion is not a matter of abstract beliefs. It does not consist in performing religious rites and ceremonies. It does not mean merely the living of a good moral life. We see here that true religion means to have daily dealings with the living God. In the heights and depths of life's experiences, He is the supreme and constant reality with which man has to do. These prayers and hymns and meditations have the authentic note of the practice of the presence of God. Moreover, the religion of the Psalms fits our human situation in its two aspects. We are individuals; each must pray with his own heart and mind. But we also are social beings, and we belong together. Our life is a shared life, and we *join* our voices in prayer and praise.

The God Who Speaks in the Psalms

The first overwhelming impression we receive from what the Psalms say to us about God is that He is the exalted Lord, master of the world which He has made, and ruler of men and nations.

> O LORD, our Lord,
> How majestic is thy name in all the earth! (Psalm 8 : 1)
> The LORD is a great God,
> and a great king above all gods.
> The sea is his, for he made it,
> and his hands formed the dry land.
> O come, let us worship and bow down,
> Let us kneel before the LORD, our maker! (Psalm 95 : 3, 5, 6)

God is the supreme Judge, of peoples, rulers and

individual men, and of the superhuman powers in the invisible world of spirit.

> The LORD judges the peoples;
> Judge me, O LORD, according to my right!(Psalm 7 : 8)
> In the midst of the gods he holds judgment. (Psalm 82 : 1)

It is made plain for all the world to see that the God who made the world still governs it, and He is good. Right, not wrong, is in control in spite of all appearances.

> Surely there is a reward for the righteous,
> Surely there is a God who judges on earth! (Psalm 58 : 11)

It is because of this confidence in the sovereign goodness and dependable justice of God that these poets pray so urgently for deliverance from cruelty and oppression. The God they worship is the mighty Champion of the oppressed, the weak, the innocent falsely accused, the hurt and the helpless.

> When the righteous cry for help, the LORD hears;
> The LORD is near to the broken-hearted,
> and saves the crushed in spirit. (Psalm 34 : 17–18)

He is the "Father of the fatherless, and protector of widows" (Psalm 68 : 5). This is in accordance with His nature,

> For the LORD is righteous, He loves right deeds,
> (but)
> His soul hates him who loves violence. (Psalm 11 : 7, 5)
> Good and upright is the LORD. (Psalm 25 : 8)

The goodness of God is seen not only in His reaction against wickedness and oppression. It is evident also in His works of creation and providence, in His gifts of life and land and food, and in His personal concern and care for His servants.

O LORD, how manifold are thy works!
In wisdom thou hast made them all;
The earth is full of thy creatures.
These all look to thee, to give them their food in due season.

(Psalm 104 : 24, 27)

The world of nature rejoices in the goodness of God:

Thou crownest the year with thy bounty;
The meadows clothe themselves with flocks,
The valleys deck themselves with grain,
They shout and sing together for joy. (Psalm 65 : 11, 13)

God's goodness is seen also by His servants in the blessings of daily life:

The LORD is my chosen portion and my cup,
Thou holdest my lot,
The lines have fallen for me in pleasant places.

(Psalm 16 : 5–6)

His love surpasses the devotion of parents:

When my father and my mother have abandoned me,
The LORD will take me in. (Psalm 27 : 10)

How does God reveal Himself to His servants? First, through the order, beauty and beneficence of the creation.

The heavens are telling the glory of God. (Psalm 19 : 1)
Thou makest springs gush forth in the valleys . . .
Thou dost cause the grass to grow for the cattle, and plants
    for man to cultivate,
That he may bring forth food from the earth.

(Psalm 104 : 10, 14)

Second, through the recollection of God's acts of revelation and deliverance in the past:

Our fathers have told us
    what deeds thou didst perform in their days;
(how)
    Thou didst set them free;
For not by their own sword did they win the land.

(Psalm 44 : 1–3)

Third, through the experience of worship:

> O send out thy light and thy truth,
> Let them lead me,
> Let them bring me to thy holy hill!
> Then will I go to the altar of God,
> To God my exceeding joy. (Psalm 43 : 3–4)

The fourth medium of the knowledge of God is the experience of His answer to man's cry of need:

> I waited patiently for the LORD;
> He inclined to me and heard my cry;
> He set my feet upon a rock;
> He put a new song in my mouth. (Psalm 40 : 1–3)

God's power, His justice and His goodness are undergirded by His faithfulness:

> I will proclaim thy faithfulness to all generations.
> (Psalm 89 : 1)

Together with this emphasis on God's exaltedness and on His goodness, we find in these testimonies of ancient faith an equal stress upon God's nearness to those who trust Him. He is immediately and deeply concerned for His servants in the everyday experience of life.

> O LORD, thou hast searched me and known me;
> Thou knowest when I sit down and when I rise;
> Thou discernest my thoughts from afar, and art aware of
>   all I do. (Psalm 139 : 1–3)

Man's relationships with such a God are not merely formal and external. They rise to the level of personal fellowship:

> How precious are thy thoughts to me, O God;
> When I awake, I am still with thee. (Psalm 139 : 17–18)

Religion reaches to the core of man's being. The last secrets of pride and pretence are uncovered, and the believer knows that he is utterly dependent on divine forgiveness and renewal:

> Behold, thou desirest truth in the inward being;
> Hide thy face from my sins,
>   and blot out all my iniquities.
> Create in me a clean heart, O God . . .
>   and take not thy holy Spirit from me.
>
> (Psalm 51 : 6, 9, 10)

God's constant guidance is known from experience:

> He makes me lie down in green pastures,
> He leads me beside still waters,
> He restores my soul. (Psalm 23 : 2–3)

Above all, He imparts strength to man's spirit:

> The LORD is my rock, my fortress and my deliverer,
> My shield . . . and my stronghold. (Psalm 18 : 2)

This unquestioned reality of God's experienced mercy makes all the more agonizing the cries for help when He is silent and seems to have withdrawn from His servant:

> How long, O LORD?
> Wilt thou forget me for ever? (Psalm 13 : 1)
> Why dost thou hide thy face?
> Rise up! Come to our help! (Psalm 44 : 24, 26)
> My God, my God, why hast thou forsaken me? (Psalm 22 : 1)

The passionate earnestness of these petitions is far removed from the easy assumption that a prayer has only to be spoken in order to be answered as man wishes. God is still God. He is not at man's beck and call. The psalmists knew that the prayer that is heard is the one which says, "Nevertheless, not my will but thine be done". Only as a man submits himself to the *hidden* God who has chosen to reveal Himself, and only as he realizes his own ignorance and emptiness apart from God, can God answer his prayer.

76

The LORD's throne is in heaven,
His eyes behold, his eyelids try the children of men.

(Psalm 11 : 4)

Out of the depths I cry to thee, O LORD!
My soul waits for the LORD more than watchmen for the
    morning. (Psalm 130 : 1, 6)
A broken and contrite heart, O God,
Thou wilt not despise. (Psalm 51 : 17)

Man's Need and God's Salvation

One of the ways in which God speaks to us to-day
through the Psalms is by reminding us of the sordidness,
emptiness and frailty of our lives apart from Him.

Know that the LORD is God!
It is he that made us, and we are his! (Psalm 100 : 3)
Forget not all his benefits . . .
For he knows our form,
He remembers that we are dust. (Psalm 103 : 2, 14)

The psalmists' cries for help rise from particular circumstances which often they describe in urgent terms.
We hear of personal and national enemies, false accusations, oppressions, sickness and other adversities. Yet
the need they express is a spiritual need rather than a
change of circumstance. They ask for courage, hope,
wisdom, guidance, loyalty, cleansing, humility, acceptance. They are lonely and afraid when confronted by
hostility and contempt, violence and defiant wickedness.
They are perplexed to see how some men prosper in
spite of their disobedience to the laws of God. The
future seems dark. They know their own weakness, and
how easy it is to fall into sin and yield to doubt. They
grow weary in the struggle:

O LORD, how many are my foes!
Many say of me, There is no help for him in God.

(Psalm 3 : 1–2)

Men attack me without cause . . .
They reward me evil for good. (Psalm 109 : 3, 5)

77

Help, LORD! for there is no longer any that is godly,
The faithful have vanished
    from among the sons of men. (Psalm 12 : 1)
Arise, O LORD! Let not man prevail!
Let the nations know that they are but men!
                                            (Psalm 9 : 19, 20)

The cry of need is at the same time a cry of faith:

My help comes from the LORD,
    who made heaven and earth. (Psalm 121 : 2)

The worshipper knows that

Against thee, thee only, have I sinned . . .
So that thou art just in thy sentence. (Psalm 51 : 4)
Because the LORD is at my right hand,
I shall not be moved;
Therefore my heart is glad and my soul rejoices,
My body also dwells secure. (Psalm 16 : 8–9)
When I am afraid, I put my trust in thee. (Psalm 56 : 3)

The greatness of man's need is the measure of God's
deliverance.

How abundant is thy goodness,
What thou hast done for those who take refuge in thee!
                                            (Psalm 31 : 19)
Thou, who hast made me see many sore troubles,
Wilt revive me again. (Psalm 71 : 20)

What is meant by "salvation" is, in the first instance,
what God does to meet man's need in a particular situation. The result is not merely, however, the grateful
memory of that moment of deliverance; it is the beginning or renewal of confidence in God. God Himself
becomes man's salvation.

God is our refuge and strength,
A proven help in trouble;
Therefore we are not afraid. (Psalm 46 : 1–2)
My shield is with God,
    who saves the upright in heart. (Psalm 7 : 10)
The LORD is my light and my salvation. (Psalm 27 : 1)

78

Nowhere is this testimony to God's saving power set forth more effectively than in the 73rd Psalm. The writer's most serious peril has been the temptation to lose confidence in God.

> My feet had almost stumbled,
> For I was envious of the arrogant. (vss. 2, 3)
> (I said)
> "In vain have I kept my heart clean". (vs. 13)
> My soul was embittered. (vs. 21)
> Yet, (though I had not realized it)
> I was continually with thee,
> Thou didst grasp my right hand;
> Thou wilt guide me with thy counsel,
>   and afterward receive me with honour. (vss. 23, 24)
> Whom have I in heaven but thee?
> With thee, I desire no other upon earth.
> My flesh and my heart fail;
> But God is my portion for ever. (vss. 25, 26)

The Meaning of Life

It was when he had gone into the sanctuary of God that this psalmist had gained illumination of the profound perplexities of his existence. As another put it:

> They feast on the abundance of thy house; . . .
> With thee is the fountain of life;
> In thy light do we see light. (Psalm 36 : 8, 9)

Light on life's problems and on life's meaning is a fruit of salvation. The psalmists share with us the light they found, as they reflected in the presence of God.

The visible world spoke to them, as we have seen, of the glory and wisdom of the Creator in whose hands the believer has placed his perplexities. The starry firmament by night and the sun by day testified to God in wordless speech (Psalm 19 : 1–6). The same God had spoken to Israel in His commandments which are— "more to be desired than gold, sweeter than honey" (Psalm 19 : 10). In the study of God's law the religious man found a happiness which the worldly man could not imagine. His spirit was refreshed as a tree is refreshed by water in a barren land (Psalm 1).

We must refer again to that other psalmist to whom the glory of the stars brought first the thought of man's insignificance and finitude, and then the wonder of God's care, and His choice of man to share His own responsibility:

> When I look at thy heavens . . .
> The moon and the stars which thou hast set in place,
> What is man, that thou dost give him a thought?
(Yet)
> Thou hast given him dominion over the works of thy hands.
>> (Psalm 8 : 3, 4, 6)

But man, who is thus honoured, lives a brief and uncertain life. He passes away and is soon forgotten. It is only when he comes to realize his mortality, and learns to rest upon God's eternal goodness, that his life gains worth and meaning:

> Like grass which is renewed in the morning . . .
(and)
> In the evening fades and withers, . . .
> The years of our life . . .
>> are soon gone, and we fly away.
(But)
> LORD, thou hast been our dwelling place in all generations,
> From of old and for ever thou art God.
>> (Psalm 90 : 5, 6, 10, 1, 2)

Death turns to dust all human pride, and

> Truly no man can ransom himself,
> Or give to God the price of his life. (Psalm 49 : 7)

Wickedness creates its own just punishment:

> The wicked conceives evil . . .
>> and falls into the pit which he has made.
>> (Psalm 7 : 14, 15)

Some of the psalmists were particularly troubled by Israel's national misfortunes and the vicissitudes of her religious history. The 44th Psalm contrasts the divine favour shown to the fathers with God's seeming indifference to a present condition of defeat and shame. Psalm 74 bewails the destruction of the temple, while God gives no sign through His prophets. Is it that God has forgotten His people? Is He angry with them? Whatever the reason, not only do His people suffer, but His name is brought into contempt.

> How long, O LORD, is the foe to scoff?
> Is the enemy to revile thy name for ever? (Psalm 74 : 10)
> How long, O LORD? Wilt thou be angry forever?
> Deliver us, and forgive our sins, for thy name's sake.
> Why should the nations say,
> Where is their God? (Psalm 79 : 5, 9, 10)

We, too, are puzzled that God should allow wars and famines and other catastrophes to happen. We wonder why there seems to be no answer to prayers for deliverance and peace. We have had in Christ a light far brighter than the psalmists knew in their days of darkness. It is wonderful that for the most part they kept the faith, and waited patiently for the Lord.

> Wilt thou not revive us again,
>   that thy people may rejoice in thee? (Psalm 85 : 6)

Faith answers:

> God will speak peace to his people;
> His salvation is near for those who fear him. (Psalm 85 : 8, 9)

The Confidence of Faith

This confidence in God as the sole security of His people in a world of turmoil and danger is the theme of that triumphant anthem, Psalm 46:

God is our refuge and strength . . .
Therefore we will not fear,
    though the earth should change,
    and the mountains shake in the heart of the sea.
The nations rage, the kingdoms totter,
He utters his voice, the earth melts.
Come, behold the works of the LORD;
He makes wars to cease to the end of the earth.
The LORD of hosts is with us,
The God of Jacob is our refuge. (Psalm 46 : 1, 2, 6, 8, 9, 11)

To the singer of Psalm 48 the towers and ramparts of Zion, the holy city, are symbols of divine protection, not only for the present but for all time to come:

Walk about Zion, go round about her,
Observe her ramparts;
That you may tell a later generation that God is here, our
    eternal God,
It is he who leads us. (Psalm 48 : 12–14)

A nation's faith is the shared confidence of the men and women who compose the nation. It is, in the life of the nation, the counterpart of the trust of the man who can sleep in peace because God is the security of his spirit:

Thou, LORD, art a shield about me . . .
I lie down and sleep, I wake again,
    for the LORD sustains me;
I am not afraid of ten thousands of people. (Psalm 3 : 3, 5, 6)

This is the blessedness of "the man who makes the LORD his trust" (Psalm 40 : 4). Hope is faith which is content to wait:

Why are you cast down, O my soul?
And why are you disquieted within me?
Hope in God, for I shall yet praise him. (Psalm 42 : 5)
I believe that I shall see the goodness of the LORD
    in the land of the living. (Psalm 27 : 13)

Such faith and hope, which are God's gifts, can be shared with others:

> Wait for the LORD;
> Be strong, and let your heart take courage! (Psalm 27 : 14)

The best testimony is the testimony of experience:

> I waited patiently for the LORD,
> He inclined to me and heard my cry.
> Many will see and fear,
>   and put their trust in the LORD. (Psalm 40 : 1, 3)

The Way of Prayer

We can learn much from the Psalms about the meaning of prayer.

First, that effective prayer requires strong faith; "whoever would draw near to God must believe that he exists and that he rewards those who seek him" (Hebrews 11 : 6).

> The LORD lives; blessed be my rock!
> Exalted be the God of my salvation! (Psalm 18 : 46)
> Our help is in the name of the LORD
>   who made heaven and earth. (Psalm 124 : 8)
> Those who trust in the LORD are like Mount Zion, which
>   cannot be moved. (Psalm 125 : 1)

Men who spoke thus knew Him in whom they had believed.

The second thing to be noted is the urgency and importunity of these prayers. We recall our Lord's parable of the unrighteous judge to whom a widow addressed her incessant petitions. The psalmists are very urgent in their prayers. They expostulate with God in words which seem almost irreverent:

> Rouse thyself! Why sleepest thou, O Lord? (Psalm 44 : 23)
> Why dost thou stand afar off, O LORD?
> Why dost thou hide thyself in times of trouble?
>   (Psalm 10 : 1)

The fact that they dare to speak in this way shows how real is their belief in God, and how sure they are that

He can answer prayer. They do not hesitate to tell God of their troubles in the most outspoken fashion:

> Answer me when I call, O God of my right!
> Be gracious to me, and hear my prayer! (Psalm 4 : 1)
> O thou my help, hasten to my aid!
> Deliver my life from the sword! (Psalm 22 : 19, 20)

The problem of unanswered prayer is acute in such circumstances.

> Be not deaf to me, lest, if thou be silent to me,
> I become like those who go down to the Pit. (Psalm 28 : 1)

Is God testing His servant, to see if his faith is strong enough to accept disappointment? Is it that the answer has been given, but has not been recognized?

> O my God, I cry by day, but thou dost not answer,
>   and by night, and find no rest. (Psalm 22 : 2)

Faith answers:

> God does not despise the affliction of the afflicted,
> He has not hid his face from him,
> But has heard, when he cried to him. (Psalm 22 : 24)

Some of the psalmists are more ready than are others to acknowledge that their own sinfulness has stood in the way of God's response:

> When I declared not my sin . . .
> Day and night thy hand was heavy upon me.
> I said, I will confess my transgression to the LORD;
> Then thou didst forgive the guilt of my sin.
>
>   (Psalm 32 : 3, 4, 5)
>
> O thou who hearest prayer,
> To thee shall all flesh come, on account of sins.
> When our transgressions prevail over us,
> Thou dost forgive them. (Psalm 65 : 2, 3)

The writer of Psalm 25 : 11 makes his appeal "for thy name's sake, O LORD". The God of Israel had a personal name (Yahweh, for which we say "the LORD").

84

His revealed nature and characteristic goodness were signified by this name, which distinguished Him from all "other gods", and which was associated with all that He had meant to Israel. The psalmist thus lays claim to God's promises, and at the same time commits himself to the good purposes of the One whose name he uses:

> Thy covenant love is before my eyes,
>   and I live daily with thy faithfulness. (Psalm 26 : 3)

Otherwise, he would have no right to ask God's aid:

> If there be wrong in my hands, . . .
> Let the enemy pursue and overtake me. (Psalm 7 : 3, 5)

Thus, self-examination as well as faith is a condition of effective prayer:

> In the day of my trouble, I seek the Lord, . . .
> I meditate and search my spirit. (Psalm 77 : 2, 6)

He who is to—

> receive blessing from the LORD,
> And vindication from his saving God,

must have—

> clean hands and a pure heart. (Psalm 24 : 5, 4)

"If I had cherished iniquity in my heart", says another poet, "the Lord would not have listened" (Psalm 66 : 18).

This commitment to God's purposes means also a humble submission to His wisdom and acceptance of His decision:

> Into thy hand I commit my spirit . . .
> I trust in thee, O LORD . . .
> My times are in thy hand. (Psalm 31 : 5, 14,15)

The worshipper seeks deeper understanding of the One to whom he prays and to whom he has dedicated his life:

> Make me to know thy ways, O LORD,
> Teach me thy paths. (Psalm 25 : 4)

He accepts gratefully a love which is deeper and wiser than any human love:

> As a father pities his children,
> So the LORD pities those who fear him.
> As the heavens are high above the earth,
> So vast is his covenant mercy toward those who reverence him.
> (Psalm 103 : 13, 11)

Prayer to such a God can never be a matter of few or many words. We are not heard for our "much speaking". The prayer of intimate communion may be in silence.

> For God alone my soul waits silently. (Psalm 62 : 1)
> Before a word is on my tongue, O LORD,
> Thou knowest it completely. (Psalm 139 : 4)

The Perfection of Praise

In the Hebrew Bible the Book of Psalms is entitled "Praises". It has been used for many centuries chiefly as a form of praise in worship, Jewish and Christian. The faith and devotion of a congregation are more naturally expressed in song than in ordinary speech. Our hearts are united when we *join* to sing. Rhythm and music add wings to our thoughts. Above all, the joy of salvation demands utterance in exultant song. Worship is adoration, and adoration is praise.

We praise God not only for His benefits, but above all for what He is. He is "worthy to be praised" (Psalm 18 : 3).

> It is good to sing praises to our God,
> For he is gracious, and a song of praise is seemly.
> (Psalm 147 : 1)

86

In Psalm 21 : 13 God's power is the theme of the song. In Psalm 33 it is His goodness, His sovereignty and His wisdom. Psalm 67 acclaims His justice and His salvation. Psalm 111 gives thanks for His works in providence and the redemption of His people. The refrain of Psalm 100 : 5 becomes the text of many other hymns of thanksgiving:

> Give thanks to him, bless his name,
> For the LORD is good,
> His gracious love endures for ever.

These praises of Israel are notably objective; the worshipper turns from himself to God:

> Bless the LORD, O my soul!
> O LORD, my God, thou art very great! (Psalm 104 : 1)
> Extol the LORD our God;
> Worship at his footstool, for he is holy! (Psalm 99 : 5)

Joy and gratitude are the keynotes of such hymns. From full hearts men praise God for both general and particular mercies. It is He:

> Who alone does great wonders,
> Who by understanding made the heavens,
> Who led his people through the wilderness,
> Who gave them a land as a heritage,
> Who remembered us in our low estate.
> (Psalm 136 : 4, 5, 16, 21, 23)

It is He also who delivers individuals from various troubles:

> Some wandered in desert wastes . . .
> Some sat in darkness and gloom (of prison) . . .
> Some were sick through their sinful ways . . .
> Some went down to the sea in ships . . .
>   and were at their wits' end.
> Then they cried to the LORD in their trouble,
>   and he delivered them from their distress.
> (Psalm 107 : 4, 10, 17, 23, 27, 28)

The anthem of praise unites all God's creatures in heaven and earth.

> Bless the LORD, O my soul,
>> and all that is within me, bless his holy name!
> Bless the LORD, O my soul,
>> and forget not all his benefits!
> Bless the LORD, O you his angels,
>> You mighty ones who do his word!
> Bless the LORD, all his hosts,
>> His ministers, who do his will!
> Bless the LORD, all his works,
>> in all places of his dominion!
> Bless the LORD, O my soul! (Psalm 103 : 1, 2, 20–22)

This is the perfection of praise!

It is echoed in the Revelation of St. John, in the song of the elders before the throne of God:

> Worthy art thou, our Lord and God,
> To receive glory and honour and power,
> For thou didst create all things,
> And by thy will they came to be and were created.
>> (Rev. 4 : 11)